TAKE IT BACK!

Library of Congress Cataloging-in-Publication Data

0Singer, Arlene,
Take it back: the art of returning almost anything
by Arlene Singer & Karen Parmet
First Edition
160 p., 15 x 23 cm
ISBN 0-915765-74-8 $9.95
1. Shopping.
2. Consumer education.
0 I. Parmet, Karen,
II. Title.
TX335.S554 1990
640'.73--dc20   90-13360

CIP

Includes index.

PRINTED IN THE UNITED STATES OF AMERICA
1991 Edition

TAKE IT BACK!

The Art of Returning *Almost* Anything

ARLENE SINGER
AND
KAREN PARMET

National
Press
Books

Dedication

This book is dedicated to our six children, whom we never would return.

Acknowledgments

We would like to thank Janet Meyerson, Jeff Parmet, Rebekah Greenwald and Joel Joseph for their assistance and support concerning this book. The following also were helpful: Autocaps, Clarence Ditlow and the Center for Auto Safety, Frank Bennett, Lana Harris, Cheri Hayes, Fred Jacoby, Terry Morrow, Consumer Product Safety Commission, Nordstrom, Syms and L.L. Bean.

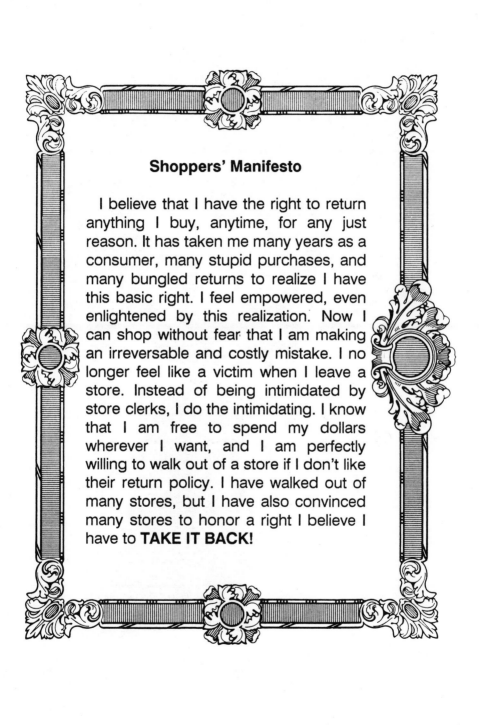

Shoppers' Manifesto

I believe that I have the right to return anything I buy, anytime, for any just reason. It has taken me many years as a consumer, many stupid purchases, and many bungled returns to realize I have this basic right. I feel empowered, even enlightened by this realization. Now I can shop without fear that I am making an irreversable and costly mistake. I no longer feel like a victim when I leave a store. Instead of being intimidated by store clerks, I do the intimidating. I know that I am free to spend my dollars wherever I want, and I am perfectly willing to walk out of a store if I don't like their return policy. I have walked out of many stores, but I have also convinced many stores to honor a right I believe I have to **TAKE IT BACK!**

Table of Contents

1

Introduction: The Cautious Consumer

Do you have a closet full of clothes you never wear? Do you have a fear of store clerks? Do you procrastinate about returning things? Do you through out sales receipts? If you experience any of these symptoms you definitely need this book. You may be suffering from "returnaphobia."

Don't worry. We probably can help you. We will offer practical tips regarding returns, including steps you can take before, as well as after your purchase, has been made.

We interviewed countless shoppers, store clerks and managers and compiled hundreds of returns stories, too many to include in this book. We've tried to highlight some examples in order to help you, the consumer, copes with today's shopping (and returning) problems. This book starts out with the authors described as "we." The rest of the book uses the first person to describe examples that one of use came across, or experienced, while preparing this book.

If you are interested in how you can save time and money and learn not to be plagued by feelings of guilt or intimidation, then this book is for you.

I found over the years that many things I bought turned out to be mistakes, particularly clothes and jewelry. I got stuck with these things—my closets and drawers are filled with them. I bought things I really didn't like, but I was always afraid to return them. Not anymore.

Your mistakes are hanging in your closet.

I have since learned to be more careful when buying and always ask questions regarding return policies. Sometimes, I'll even ask the salesperson to write on my sales receipt that the item is returnable. Also, I keep my sales receipts organized and in one place for easy access. As soon as I get home, I carefully remove the tags or proof of purchase from whatever I've bought and pin them to the sales receipt.

I am a person who loves something in the store and then hates it when I get it home. Sometimes I'll wear a blouse or a dress only to discover that it does not look as good as it did in the store, or that it doesn't go well with the shoes I bought it to match. Maybe that sweater the sales person told me was "extra-soft wool" feels itchy against my skin, or the color fades when I hand wash it. Any number of reasons can make me wish I never bought something, especially if I listened to store advertising.

Most people believe that after you wear clothing, "that's it," no returning. This is not the case. While I certainly do not advocate returning something you have worn because you ruined it, I have returned many things after wearing or using them for any of a number of reasons, or because they don't do what they were advertised to do. It's my prerogative. Why should I keep a girdle that doesn't gird, or energized pantyhose that sag in the first hour I wear them?

My research shows that most consumers keep things they have a legal right to return. Unfortunately, stores know this and actively discourage returns, hoping a consumer will keep merchandise that is poorly made, or misrepresented by manufacturers and advertising, rather than go through the hassle of returning. Unfair management cannot stop the educated consumer, however, so if you've been duped, **TAKE IT BACK!** It really is quite easy.

Most major department stores have liberalized their return policies in recent years. However, you still have to be careful, especially when shopping in small boutiques and shops. Some will write, "final sale" on your receipt without telling you. Some have signs that say you can only return within seven days and then only for store credit. Watch out for these stores. I learned the hard way.

I try to avoid these stores like the plague, but sometimes they have something unique that I can't find anywhere else. I have found that in these stores you can negotiate a compromise. For example, I tell them I want to buy it, take it home, try it on, show my husband, and then if he doesn't like it, I'll bring it back the same day. This technique has never failed.

I have also learned that I should absolutely love something before buying it, because if I don't I will never learn to love it later. Even if I love something, I've trained myself to walk right out of the store if they won't assure me that I can change my mind and take it back. In such cases I now say, "Since you don't take returns I will go somewhere else." This technique, more often than not, puts the proprietor in a negotiating mood. Then I know I've got him!

Always ask about a store's return policy before making your purchase.

Return Policy Questions

☐ **What is their return policy?**

☐ **Is there a time limit for returns?**

☐ **Will I get a refund or only store credit?**

☐ **Is "all sales final" stamped on your receipt or posted in the store?**

NOTE: Always use credit cards instead of checks. Usually, stores make you wait 10 days for the check to clear before they will issue a refund. (We don't advocate abusing your credit, but using credit cards gives you additional protection that other means of payment do not provide.)

If return restrictions apply, and you find them to be as offensive as I do, tell the store manager! Negotiate a compromise that you can live with. If you are met with resistance (or a clerk who just doesn't care), walk out! You have rights as a consumer. Exercise them!

⇒ Exercising Your Rights

The right to **"TAKE IT BACK"** belongs to all consumers. If you don't exercise this right when a product is unsatisfactory, you are not only doing yourself a disservice you are doing the retailer and manufacturer a disservice. Stores and manufacturers need to know when their quality is failing, when their products are dangerous or defective. When you buy a product you are voting with your wallet. When you return unacceptable products you are voting against the product. At the same time you are cleaning out your closets and drawers and fattening your wallet.

In this book, I will share my experiences and my know-how with you. I will provide tips for a successful return, and help you to be a responsible consumer. By following step-by-step suggestions, you will gain the organization and lobbying power necessary to make store managers listen. You will no longer be slave to quick decisions that diminish your checking account balance with no pleasure in return. I guarantee if you only learn to recognize your rights, you will enjoy shopping more and you will save money.

➠ Give Returnable Gifts

A good way to begin exercising your own rights is to help others exercise theirs. When you buy someone a gift keep in mind the possibility that the recipient might not like it. For this reason you should make it easy for the gift to be returned. This insures that your gift will be used and appreciated, so while the price tag should be removed from your gift, other tags should be left on, and the store's name should appear either on the tag or on the box.

When buying gifts for friends and relatives in distant cities it is a good idea to stick to big name stores. I always shop at a store that has a branch located right in the recipient's home town. Some stores, like Sears, Wards, Toys-R-Us, and The Limited are located in nearly every part of the country and are used to making returns for items bought in other cities. Mail order houses like Spiegel and L.L. Bean return gifts from their catalogs without question.

➠ Don't Throw Away Broken or Defective Products

The best way to start on the road to responsible consumerism is by dealing with products you already have. If a toy breaks leaving exposed jagged edges my first reaction is to throw it away so that my children and their friends are not injured. I know that toys designed for children should not break however, and even if they do they should not become dangerous weapons in innocent hands. Even if toys have been used for years they should not become dangerous. This is why instead of throwing a defective product away I take it back to the store where I bought it. This sends the store and the manufacturer a message. I will tell you later how to go about having stores take back dangerous and defective products even if they were bought seasons ago.

▥➡ In the Know

Knowing your shopper's rights is the first step towards enhancing your return power, and shopping at the right place is the second. A lot of products you never thought could be returned most definitly can and should be taken back. Raise your expectations, you deserve the quality you pay for. Imagine how much more money you would have if only you knew to **TAKE IT BACK!**

2
You Can Return Almost Anything

Everything is returnable. If you are unhappy with a product that does not live up to its advertising claims you have every right to take it back. Here are some examples:

☞ When a Rose is not a Rose

I was walking out of the supermarket one day when I saw a casual acquaintance carrying a bag of dead roses. I couldn't imagine in my wildest dreams why anyone would be carrying a bag of dead roses. She said that she was on her way to the florist to return them. They had been given to her by her boyfriend and they "died" a few days later. I asked her if I could tag along to the floral shop and observe the store's reaction. "This I gotta see," I said to myself. We walked into the floral shop together and she showed the dead roses to the clerk. She said that her boyfriend was furious that the roses didn't last a week and that for $60 he didn't get his money's worth. Five minutes later we walked out with a dozen fresh long-stemmed roses.

☞ Back to the Grocery Store

Supermarkets are usually very receptive to accepting returns. I have taken many food products back, either when an item was spoiled, or when I no longer needed it. If a product spoils before the date marked on the package don't be ashamed to return it on your next shopping trip.

My cat, who is now getting old, was given a special diet by his veterinarian. I returned the unused cans of his old cat food to the supermarket and they accepted them without question. As long as the canned or packaged goods you return are not damaged or opened, the store will almost always accept them.

When my children decided that they would no longer eat a certain brand of pizza sauce I returned the remaining cans. Have you ever stocked up on a particular brand of food for a house guest, and found some left six month later collecting dust? Don't be shy—**TAKE IT BACK!**

☞ When You're Swimming in Your Suit

Most personal items, such as bathing suits and underwear, are not returnable unless the original packaging has not been disturbed. This is understandable, I would not want to buy bikini bottoms that have been worn by another person either. On the other hand, sometimes in a store you just can't tell what looks good, or even what fits. Now with the aid of disposable adhesive panty protectors, if you prefer trying on a suit in the comfort of your own home, you can order one. Many mail order houses accept returns of personal garments with no questions asked, as long as the adhesive protector is still on. I had no trouble·returning a bathing suit to Spiegel that did not fit properly. Spiegel is particularly good with returns because it even pays return postage.

☞ The Meltdown

My husband can be a pain in the kitchen. He overheated a Cuisinart pot and it melted all over my stove. A pot made for cooking should not melt, even when used by a clumsy husband. I pointed my husband in the direction of Bloomingdales to return the very expensive cookware. Bloomingdales refused to exchange the pot for a new one claiming that the cookware had been abused. My husband protested that the pot had not been dropkicked, it was used for cooking, and that a pot made for cooking should not melt when used on an ordinary stove. The clerk was adamant.

My husband refused to take no for an answer. He took the melted down pot to another Bloomingdales store where they exchanged it for another pot. The lessons to be learned here are one: don't let your husband cook with your expensive cookware and two: don't take no for an answer, try another branch of the store where the item was purchased.

☞ Dining Maligned

It is often embarrassing to return a dish ordered in a restaurant. Since restaurant prices are often very high, you must balance the slight embarrassment against the feeling that you did not receive what you ordered. I must admit that I rarely complain in restaurants—I go out to eat to enjoy myself, not to complain about food. However, I recently ordered a bowl of clam chowder that was served containing no clams at all. I promptly returned it. At another restaurant I ordered a glass of wine that was undrinkable. I explained to the waitress that the wine smelled peculiar and she replaced it with a glass of a different wine.

☞ Shoe Leather

I attempted, without success, to return a pair of shoes that did not wear well to a small shoe store. The shoe store claimed that the wear was normal "wear and tear" and that they could do nothing about it. On the other hand I know someone who has returned work shoes to Sears after wearing them for a year. Sears replaced the shoes without any sour expression.

☞ Home Furnishings

Many shoppers will often pick out several different pillows to highlight their living room couch. If the colors don't match they then return the offending pillow. You should not hesitate to do the same for pillows, ready-made curtains and other home furnishings **so long as the item was not custom made for you.**

Acceptions to this rule do occur. I purchased two matching DelMar shades many years ago. After using the shades for at least five years, one of the mechanisms failed. I called the store where I purchased them and they arranged with DelMar to replace the broken shade. When the new one was delivered the color did not match the old shade. The two different colored shades looked horrible together. I called the DelMar representative who promptly ordered, with no charge to me, two new shades.

☞ Concert Tickets

Even concert tickets are exchangeable! I have exchanged theater tickets the day before the event. Sometimes things that are beyond your control, i.e. illness, or the death of a friend or relative force you to miss an event that you have planned for long in advance. Don't be afraid to ask for tickets to a different concert or even a future event. Your exchange may enable someone to get last minute tickets to a show that was "sold out."

☞ Lemon Aid

Did you ever have a car that was such a sour lemon, that you wanted to take it back to the car dealer? Sometimes a new car that is a real pain in the crankcase is returnable. See Chapter Eight if your car is such a lemon that you want to take it back.

Some auto manufacturers are promoting the fact that their products are returnable. Oldsmobile has recently promoted a program that gives unhappy buyers the right to a credit. The problem is that the credit is only good on another Oldsmobile.

Volkswagen has taken the concept one step further. Volkswagen Passat buyers have three months or 3,000 miles to decide whether the car meets their expectations. If buyers are unhappy with the performance of the Passat they can receive a full refund of the purchase price.

☞ No Sale is Really Final

Even if you purchase something as a "final sale," it may still be returnable. After a major snow storm, I was having no luck finding snowpants for my children. After searching an entire afternoon, I finally found some in an exclusive children's store. The snowpants were really a snowsuit with the jacket missing. The sales clerk told me I could have the snowpants for half price, but as a final sale. In my desperation, I bought them. On my way home I stopped at one more store and, of course, found exactly what I was really looking for—better quality snowpants for a cheaper price. As this pair was also offered as a final sale my option were as follows:

❶ Take the path of least resistance and keep the snowpants that I already bought;

❷ Buy the snowpants I had just found, then try to take the others back. If I could not take those back, afterwards I would try to return these (and maybe get stuck with two pairs); or

❸ Put these on "hold," go back to the other store, see if I could return those, and then buy these.

(No one ever said that being a smart shopper is easy!)

Of course I chose number three. Being the smart shopper that I am, when I went to the other store I directly asked for the manager. I explained I had bought the pants as a final sale an hour ago, but found better quality snowpants for less money. Without any hesitation, the manager accepted the return.

The two morals of this story are simple. First, don't believe everything you read. Most stores want to treat customers fairly and reasonably, so if something is fair and reasonable they will try to accommodate you. Second, ask and ye shall receive. **You can't return something if you don't try.**

☞ Open Your Eyes

Believe in the unbelievable, try the impossible. There are a few options you may not have considered. You might get treated with respect. The honest and direct approach might work best. As a consumer you have the right to satisfaction, and if you are not satisfied, let someone know, remember–**ALMOST ANYTHING CAN BE RETURNED.**

3

Reasons
for
Returns

Before returning merchandise you should have a valid reason for making the return. You need a valid reason for two purposes: **one**–for the store and **two** –for yourself. The salesperson accepting a return needs to fill out a return form and most forms include a space for the reason. There are nearly endless justifiable reasons for making returns, but to minimize embarrassment, you should have one in mind before taking an item back to a store.

L.L. Bean, one of the nation's largest mail order companies, happens to have an exemplary return policy. Bean states: "Return anything purchased from us at anytime." If the product is not 100% satisfactory in every way, they add "We will replace it, refund your purchase price or credit your credit card, as you wish. We do not want you to have anything from L.L. Bean that is not completely satisfactory." Bean lists 31 reasons for returns, including the first nine listed on the next page.

Reasons for Returns

❶ Doesn't fit properly;

❷ Faded or bled;

❸ Color wrong or did not coordinate;

❹ Defective;

❺ Arrived too late;

❻ Parts missing;

❼ Returning a gift;

❽ Changed mind; Don't like it;

❾ Ordered two or more, returning one; and

❿ For a lower price.

Other examples of good reasons to return merchandise will help you understand your rights as a consumer, and they will reinforce the feeling that you are "doing the right thing." Keep in mind that you are doing the store, and your fellow consumers a service by pointing out unacceptable products.

❖ Poor Fit

Some of us spend hours and hours searching for the "right" clothes. We strives for the perfect fit, yet whenever she tries on a purchase later at home it almost never fits right. Unable to afford keeping un-wearable clothing, we find again and again that we have to deal with a "return trip" to the store.

Improper fit is certainly a bona fide reason to return clothing. It isn't always easy to tell if something fits well while you are in the dressing room. You may be tired, the lighting may be poor or the mirror may distort your appearance. Once you are home, things often look different. You may also have the opinion of a roommate or spouse, which is not always available on a shopping trip.

Shoes are especially difficult to fit. Nordstrom is one store who will take back any shoe, even after it's been worn. It is definitely worth a try at other stores as well. My friend Betty tried to wear a pair of new shoes for two weeks and she was miserable. She took them back to the major department store where she had purchased them, explained her situation, and sure enough, they refunded her purchase price.

It is usually not a problem to send back an item ordered from a catalog because it fits poorly. Most clothing catalogs state their return policies and procedures on their order form. Because I've had difficulties in ordering the proper size, I have discovered that I could even return a bathing suit, usually an impossibility in a retail store.

Even toys can have a "poor fit." Many toys carry labels recommending an appropriate age group. Manufacturers can make gross errors, however, as in the case of a model airplane bought by my friend. Recommended for 7 to 8 year olds, this engineer daddy felt the airplane was overly complex for adults to assemble. He managed to return it, half-assembled, on the grounds that the label was misleading. The manager agreed, and my friend was happy that he and his son could attempt to build an easier model.

❖ Damaged or Defective Merchandise

Any damaged or defective purchases should be returned immediately. This applies to appliances, electronic equipment, furniture, clothing and so forth. Occasionally, you may run into problems, particularly if the disfunction appears after some time. In these situations, it is important to fight for your rights. It was your hard-earned money which bought the item and you should be satisfied with it.

A defect may not be known for a long time, but this does not mean you can't replace it or have it repaired at no charge to you. For example, I bought a VCR which broke down after having worked perfectly for four months. The written warranty was only good for ninety days, but the store replaced the VCR because it contained a defective part. See chapter ten for more detailed information about product warranties.

I had an incident with a small boutique about a damaged "final sale" item. After I brought home a rayon blouse I discovered a hole caused by an improperly inserted plastic price tag. A store clerk had carelessly "stapled" the price tag to the sleeve. I attempted to make a return. I felt that the blouse should have been marked "damaged" so that I would have been aware of the defect before I made a final purchase. No one advised me about the hole, possibly because they were unaware of it. I pointed this out to the store owner, who apparently did not agree with me. She was even rude and unapologetic. I persisted, really just wanting her to agree with me and possibly deduct a few dollars from the purchase price to compensate me for the defect. She finally begrudgingly agreed to issue a store credit.

My only recourse in this case was not to shop at this woman's boutique again. Her rudeness lost a customer, but I learned valuable lessons. From this episode I learned these:

Returning Tips

❶ Be careful shopping in **small boutiques**, which often have inflexible return policies;

❷ Always be on the lookout for **damaged** goods; and

❸ Beware of **final sale** items.

❖ Food

Food items can be returned to a supermarket or a smaller market with a valid reason. A few main reasons may be:

☐ **Spoiled items**—After opening a package of chicken or beef and discovering it smells bad, or looks like it may be spoiled, you can return it if it is within the limits of its expiration date.

☐ **Mistakes**—After returning home from a trip to the grocery you may discover that you picked up the wrong item. Just save it until your next trip and take it back.

☐ **Unused Goods**—You may have bought an item, that you generally do not use, for a house guest. Or you may have bought three cans of a product, tried one, and it tasted lousy. Return the unopened packages or cans on your next shopping trip.

Don't be embarrassed to return unused or spoiled food items. The markets will be pleased to satisfy their customers since you will be back again. If you don't need the money, donate your unused (but not spoiled) canned or packged food to a shelter or for a food drive. It doesn't do anybody any good if you throw it away, or if it stays unused on your shelves.

❖ **Disappointing Goods**

Certain items can be returned, even after they are used, simply because you are dissappointed in them. You may feel uncomfortable doing this, so proper judgment must be exercised in this area. Unfortunately, some people abuse this right—as in the case of someone who wears a formal dress once and then returns it.

One example of disappointing merchandise that I

successfully returned concerns cosmetics. A few years ago I was enticed by a new type of Estee Lauder lipstick which was advertised as a "conditioning formula." The lipstick did not work for me as promoted, it caked up on my lips terribly. After a considerable amount of time, I realized that I was not using it, and since it was quite expensive, I decided to return it. The sales person at the department store where I purchased the lipstick was very accommodating and took it back without a problem. I had a similar experience with an Estee Lauder nail polish that did not look like the color sample in the store. This was also taken back with a smile.

This may not work with less expensive cosmetics bought in the supermarket or drug store, but it seems not to be a problem in department stores. Most of the cosmetic counters in department stores which feature a single manufacturer (like Estee Lauder, Elizabeth Arden, Clinique or Lancome) are run by the cosmetic company directly, and want to satisfy their customers. If you have tried a product and are not completely satisfied, I definitely recommend taking it back, explaining why you are unsatisfied.

❖ Returning Gifts

Don't be too intimidated to return an item just because it was not purchased by you. In my opinion it is not improper to return a gift, although it may be awkward. The gift-giver usually wants the recipient to be happy and should expect the possibility of a return. (Tips for gift givers are provided in Chapter Nine).

It is not in good taste to hand over a receipt with a gift, but if you suspect there may be a problem you can certainly offer it. Most stores will generally take back a gift without a receipt and issue a store credit or an exchange, but they will not generally give a cash refund. Sometimes if an item has gone on sale after it was purchased, without a receipt, a store will give credit for the sale price only.

If you are trying to return a gift, and run into problems because you don't have the receipt, you should try your best to be patient with the store, and if all else fails, keep the gift. It is not proper to ask the gift giver for a receipt if it was not offered.

This also applies to a prize, which is in essence a gift. If you are lucky enough to win a prize, it can sometimes be exchanged for something else, or returned for cash so that you may purchase something that you need.

❖ Color

Rita's living room was almost decorated. It took her two years of renovation, shopping, hard work, and it cost her thousands of dollars. On a spontaneous shopping trip she found the perfect accent table to fit beside the brightly colored sofa. When she brought the table home, it looked awful, the colors clashed. Since this was a regularly priced item she had every right to return it. If it had been a final sale, she would have had to consider more carefully before bringing it home. This "perfect" buy could have been a painful mistake.

Unless you are shopping with a fabric sample, many items can only be color checked once they are brought home, particularly if they were purchased to match something. This holds especially true for clothing and shoes. Be careful! colors may not actually be what they seem in your mind.

It is very important to take your time when purchasing expensive items, or choosing a color which you may have to live with for a while. If you are unhappy with the color of an automobile there is not much you can do about it (except repaint the car).

❖ Better Price

If an item goes on sale after you purchased it for the regular price, or if you find the same item elsewhere for a lower price, and if you are concerned with saving money, by all means **TAKE IT BACK!**

Many stores will refund the difference if an item is purchased and soon thereafter goes on sale. If the store refuses, take the item back, and repurchase it at the sale price.

Some stores guarantee the lowest prices in town. If you find that another store is advertising the item that you purchased for less, bring the ad and your receipt into the store where you made the purchase, and ask for a refund of the difference. If the store refuses, take the item back and buy it at the other store.

The key thing to remember is not to get carried away with this. First, figure out how much money you will be saving. If it is not very much, weigh it against the time and energy you will be expending to return it. For many people even a small savings will be worth your effort. If the amount is considerable it will definitly be worth the effort. After all, you can use that money towards something else and with today's high cost of living, why not get the best value?

❖ Buy Two, Take One Back

When you are having difficulty choosing between two sweaters, or two door mats, buy both of them. The lighting in stores is often muted. A certain color in the store might look completely different at home. After trying the colors on in your own room or seeing them in your home, you can decide which one to keep and which one to take back.

❖ Important Things to Remember

There are many valid reasons for returning things. As I mentioned, L.L. Bean provides 31 reasons. Of course, you can come up with others based on your own judgment.

The most general reason is that you just "changed your mind." Within proper limitations you, as the consumer, have every right to be satisfied with a product and if you are not you don't have to keep it.

When you go to return an item, your trip will be easier if you:

<u>**Keep These Things in Mind**</u>

✓ **Do not be abusive of store policies;**

✓ **Keep receipts and proof of purchase;**

✓ **Try to be polite and calm;**

✓ **Tell the truth;**

✓ **The purchase is only a material item.
It is not catastrophic if it has to be kept;**

✓ **If you are embarrassed about the real reason
(need money), give a general reason;**

✓ **Most stores want a satisfied customer.**

4
Ten Tips for a Successful Return

Now that you know the protocol, it's time for strategy. Here are ten tips that will virtually guarantee a quick and hassle-free return:

❶ Know Your Reasons For Returning

Some people think they have to make up a long and complicated story about why they want to return something. This is unnecessary and only adds to the sense of discomfort returning causes us. A better approach is to be honest and direct. Stick to the facts, for example, it did not fit properly, or you already have one. In the last chapter I reviewed many valid reasons for returning purchases, and stressed that you should always have one in mind before you arrive at the store. To help you with this process, try preparing a "return plan" using one of the forms beginning at page 108. The return plan will help you to articulate your reason(s) for returning, especially if you are in a hurry or being given a hard time at the store.

When you go to the store to make the return, stick to your return plan. Be honest, truthful and direct. If you are worried your reason will be rejected, consider this return story we heard from a longtime Nordstrom salesman: "An elderly gentleman came into the store with a rumpled wool overcoat. He said he wanted to return it. I asked him why and he told me that he has been wearing it every winter day for the past three years but never really liked it." We asked the salesman what he did. "Took it back, of course," he replied. We were amazed, the man had worn the coat for three years, surely he had gotten his money's worth. Why on earth would you take it back now, we asked? "This is Nordstrom. We do what the customer wants," was his answer.

❷ Save Proof of Purchases

It is a good idea to save all sales receipts and to organize them for quick retrieval. It is easiest to return merchandise with a receipt, but if you can't find one for something you want to take back, don't give up hope. There are other ways of proving where you bought an item and how much you paid for it. If you charged the item and have your charge statement, it will include the store code, date and amount of purchase. Even if you've lost your statement the credit card company can quickly reproduce a copy for you.

❸ Charge It

The fact is, charging gives you more "return leverage." This means, if a store refuses to honor a reasonable return request, you can threaten to withhold payment. Because such action can result in a merchant complaining to your credit reporting company, this tactic should be used only after you have consulted with the credit reporting company's rules and regulations. Normally, a good faith dispute between you, the consumer, and a merchant should not hurt your credit rating.

❹ Return Merchandise Promptly and in Good Condition

Once you have decided to return something, don't let too much time pass. Some stores limit the amount of time from date of purchase that they will accept returns. For example, a store may post a sign: "all returns must be made within seven days of purchase." Also, you should return the merchandise in good condition. Make sure it is clean, folded, polished or whatever, and that it is carefully repackaged—in the original bag or box if possible.

❺ Vote with your Wallet

By voting with your wallet I mean shop at stores that have favorable return policies. Nordstrom Department Stores are an excellent example, they have single-handedly just about redefined the meaning of retailing. Their near obsession with customer service, including no-hassle returns, has forced the competition to follow suit.

Whether you are shopping at Nordstrom's or elsewhere, make it a habit to ask about a store's return policy. We have found a very wide disparity among stores between good and bad policies. Generally, larger department stores are more liberal than small shops, though this is not always the case. Cast your vote. If you find the return policy to be distasteful, tell the store manager you will be shoping elsewhere, and why.

❻ Don't Feel Guilty

Returning merchandise is neither illegal, nor immoral. Yet because so many people feel guilty or intimidated (see Chapter Five) about returning unwanted items, they keep them. You can find such items hanging in closets or tucked away in the backs of drawers. It is difficult to discard such things because they are new, yet still they remain unwanted and unused.

The fact is, consumers are far more often the victims of sales and marketing schemes and media hype than are the manufacturers and stores who push their merchandise on them. This is why so many consumer protection laws have been passed in recent years. On the other hand, we are aware of no laws designed to protect merchants from consumers!

If you still feel guilty, remember that:

➠ The store can resell merchandise returned in good condition. Used or damaged merchandise usually can be returned to suppliers for credit.

➠ Losses stores incur for merchandise that can't be sent back represent a legitimate cost of doing business. Such losses are, in fact, already figured into the price of the merchandise. In other words, you are actually paying for the right to return. So exercise it!

➐ Deal with the Person in Charge

A friend of mine recently told me a sad return story. She bought a pair of shoes in an exclusive little shop. As she was in a hurry, even though she knew they were expensive, she did not bother to ask the price. She signed the charge slip without looking at the amount. When she got home, she nearly fainted when she saw "$800" on the charge slip! My friend is fairly well off, but even she started perspiring when she thought of the idea of an $800 pair of shoes.

In amazement, she turned around and went right back to the store. She had not worn the shoes. They were in their original box. She had her receipt and charge slip. No policy limiting returns was posted in the store nor printed on the sales slip. But the sales clerk told my friend that the shoes were not returnable. Understandably, she became very upset, but left the store with the shoes which to this day sit in her closet, unworn.

When I heard this story, I was upset too. No store should treat its customers so unfairly. What did my friend do wrong by wanting to return an $800 pair of shoes? Certainly the store should have taken the shoes back. Now, my friend is so angry that she vows never to shop there again. In addition, she has made everyone she knows swear on their lives that we won't shop there either.

There are two return lessons in this story. The first and most obvious lesson is that you should never buy anything without asking the price first. Even though my friend failed to ask (a mistake, I suspect, she will never repeat), she should not have given up so quickly. The second lesson is, never accept what a store clerk tells you as true if it is so unreasonable. Ask to speak to the manager! Store clerks often do not have the authority to accept a return.

❽ Don't Take "No" For An Answer

Persistence pays! Don't take "no" for an answer. If my friend had only pushed to speak to the manager, I am certain she would have been treated more fairly. Most stores want their customers to be satisfied. Be calm and firm, and eventually you should succeed.

Remember that even a sales clerk's attitude can have a significant impact on your return. Just like you, they have their good days and their bad days. Maybe the clerk just got laid off with two weeks left, or maybe he or she is just in a bad mood. Whatever the case may be, an individual's mood should not affect the service you recieve, or your right to return.

❾ Be Prepared To Compromise

While you may not always get exactly what you would like for a return, you will get satisfaction faster and easier if you are flexible and willing to compromise. For example, some stores offer only credit on returns, not cash refunds. Here's an example:

While vacationing at a small town in North Carolina, my husband and I bought a couple of inexpensive beach umbrellas at a local general store. When we tried to put them in the sand, one of the umbrella poles snapped. The fact is, they were rather flimsy, so my husband and I decided to take them both back. Of course, when we were buying the umbrellas, we failed to ask the store's return policy (be a vigilant consumer, even when you are on vacation!). But we did have our sales receipt and it was the same day.

We walked into the store with both umbrellas in hand and announced to the store manager that we were returning them. When all of the customers and employees turned around to look, we suspected that returning things in a small beach town in North Carolina was newsworthy. The manager, who was very nice, said that we could return the broken one, but we would have to keep the other unless, of course, it broke too. Rather than go back to the beach, break the other pole, and bring it back again (our vacation was only one week and we certainly did not want to spend it in this store), we decided it was time to negotiate. In the end, we returned the broken umbrella and exchanged the good one for a sturdy rental type—one with a thick wood pole. The result:

- ☐ We got a refund (though smaller than we would have liked);

- ☐ We got an umbrella;

- ☐ We did not get burned by the sun;

- ☐ We did not spend our entire vacation in the store.

⑩ Know Your Legal Rights

Let's face it, most consumers are not lawyers, and cannot afford one to represent them, in a dispute over a merchandise return. Nonetheless, every consumer should be aware of his/her basic rights. If the item doesn't work, the manufacturer's warranty usually provides for repairs at no charge. If a repair is inconvenient or impractical, the merchant should exchange it for a new one or refund your money. Even if you are told there is no manufacturer's warranty, remind the store clerk or manager that under the law there is an "implied warranty."

This unwritten warranty is the understanding that

the product will do what it's supposed to do. If its clothing, its supposed to fit and look good on you, too! Chapter Six explains warranties in more detail.

Conclusion

If you follow these ten tips you will become an expert at making returns. To summarize the ten tips once again:

❶ **Know your reasons for returning;**

❷ **Save proof of purchases;**

❸ **Charge it;**

❹ **Return merchandise promptly and in good condition;**

❺ **Vote with your wallet;**

❻ **Don't feel guilty ;**

❼ **Deal with the person in charge;**

❽ **Don't take "no" for an answer;**

❾ **Be prepared to compromise;**

❿ **Know your legal rights.**

5

Are You Suffering From Returnaphobia?

Why is it that people buy things they don't want and keep things they would prefer to return? There are several personality types that avoid returns at all costs. I call these people returnaphobes. Returnaphobes come in four different varieties: straight-laced, macho, guilt-ridden and wimpy.

✎ The Straight-Laced Shopper

A good friend of mine, who was very well bred, absolutely refuses to return anything. Recently, she bought a dress that she hated the minute she got home. When I asked her why she didn't take it back she replied, "I was brought up to follow the rules. If I make a mistake, then it is my mistake and I should pay for it."

I call this friend the straight-laced shopper, because there is something in her upbringing that prevents her from returning. My straight-laced friend has a closet full of expensive clothes she never wears.

✎ The Macho Mentality

Macho shoppers never make mistakes. At least they never admit to any. Taking something back requires, at times, admitting you made a mistake. Thus, the macho shopper never returns anything. If you know a man or woman who avoids returning because, "it would make me feel totally stupid," then you know a macho returnaphobe.

✎ The Guilt-Ridden Type

I was shopping with another friend of mine recently

who tried on several outfits. Though she was not sure she liked any of the outfits, because she spent so much time in the store, she felt she had to buy at least one. When we got out of the store she said, "I am not sure I really like that outfit. Why did I buy it?" I asked her, "Why don't you turn around and take it back right now?" The answer: "Oh, I couldn't do that. What if the salesperson has to give back the commission? What if they can't resell the outfit? They were so nice to me. It would be wrong to return this."

My friend bought the outfit because she felt guilty and then refused to return the outfit on the basis of the exact same guilt. She is the classic guilt-ridden returnaphobe.

✎ The Wimpy Wonder

I asked many people about their return habits. The survey showed that the single biggest reason people avoid returning something, even if they would like to, is that they are afraid someone will say "no." That's right. They worry themselves to death that some sixteen-year-old-wet-behind-the-ears clerk is going to reject them. "What would I do if they say no?" Or worse, "What if they give me an argument?"

Some people avoid confrontations in stores at all costs. Even the possibility of one, which it turns out, is remote. These people, whom I call Wimpy Wonders, waste more time worrying what will happen, than it takes to make a return. Our research showed that a polite request to return or exchange an item for almost any reasonable reason (and for many not so reasonable ones) is usually met with a courteous desire to please the customer, and a prompt return.

✎ Symptoms of the Disease

Returnaphobia is a common, but treatable disease. Here are some early warning signs of returnaphobia:

The Symptoms

☐ A closet full of clothes you never wear;

☐ Fear of store clerks;

☐ Deciding you want to return something, but procrastinating about it for months;

☐ Throwing away sales receipts because you know you'll never need them.

If you suffer from returnaphobia you are not alone. Millions of Americans suffer from this malady. It can be overcome and since you are reading this book you have already taken your first step to recovery.

✏ Returning Means Never
Having to Say You're Sorry

Returnaphobia can be cured. I used to suffer horribly from this disease. The thought of returning something started my heart pounding and my palms sweating. My closets were full of mistakes—brand new clothes that I hated and never wore. But I beat it. I overcame returnaphobia. Instead of being intimidated by store clerks, it is I who does the intimidating. If you follow these simple steps, you too can overcome this dreaded disease.

1. Write your reason for your return. In Chapter Three many valid reasons for returning merchandise are listed. Think about why you are returning something first. Once you convince yourself that your reason for a return is a proper one, you will feel better about following through with it.

2. Know their return policy. (In Chapter Nine return policies are explored in detail.) Find out what the return policy of the store where you bought the item is. Knowing the policy may end your concerns. For example, if the store policy provides that you can return for any reason within seven days so long as you bring the receipt back, you can avoid unnecessary embarrassment by complying with these procedures. Knowledge of the store's policy will also empower you if you encounter a misinformed store clerk.

3. Practice. Like most things, you will get better with practice. Practice builds your confidence by providing you with the experience needed to deal with a variety of situations. Practice returning in stores with the most liberal return policies. Pretty soon, you will be tackling the more difficult boutiques and discount stores.

4. Rehearse. Part of practice is rehearsing. If you are not ready to try your return in a real store, prepare a return speech and rehearse it with a friend who can play the store clerk's role.

5. Plan. In Chapter Ten there is a return planning form. This form is designed to allow you to organize all of the information you will need for a successful return. It provides space for information about the purchase (item, store, date of purchase, price, method of payment). It provides space for you to list your reasons for returning. It is an aid to help you through the return process.

6. Take a Friend With You. Sometimes all you need is a friend to help you make a return. He or she will provide moral support, encouragement and guidance.

I have recorded three typical return conversations. Eavesdrop on them and see how return problems can be resolved to everyone's satisfaction.

✎ My Husband Doesn't Like the Dress

In a large department store . . .

<u>Customer</u>: **❝I am returning this dress. Here is my sales receipt.❞**

<u>Clerk</u>: **❝What is your reason for returning it?❞**

<u>Customer</u>: **❝My husband thinks I look like a bag lady in it.❞**

Clerk: "It appears that this dress has been worn."

Customer: "It is in the same condition as when I purchased it."

Clerk: "Well . . . Okay . . . I'll take it back . . . but only for store credit."

Customer: "I would like a cash refund."

Clerk: "According to your receipt you paid with a Visa card."

Customer: "Then I want it credited to my Visa account, not a store credit."

Clerk: "That requires a lot of paperwork."

Customer: "Do you think now is a good time to

call the store manager over?**"**

Clerk: **"**Oh, all right. I'll credit your Visa account.**"**

✎ I Already Have One of These

In a small boutique . . .

Customer: ❝I am returning this necklace. It was a gift from my boyfriend. I already have one just like it.❞

Clerk: ❝You don't have a receipt?❞

Customer: ❝No, I said it was a gift.❞

Clerk: ❝What is your boyfriend's name?❞

Customer: ❝Why do you need to know that?❞

Clerk: ❝We only accept returns for seven days. So I have to look in our files to determine when it was purchased.❞

Customer: ❝His name is Louis Lasagna.❞

Clerk: ❝I know Mr. Lasagna. . . . . This necklace

was purchased two months ago!❞

Customer: ❝I only received it for a Christmas present yesterday.❞

Clerk: ❝All right. I'll let you exchange it. Do you see something you like?❞

Customer: ❝Yes. That's fine. I'll pick out a pair of earrings instead.❞

✎ This VCR Doesn't Work

In a specialty electronics store . . .

Customer: ❝My VCR does not work properly. I want a new one. Here is my receipt.❞

Clerk: ❝What's wrong with it.❞

Customer: ❝It ejects the tapes when it is

supposed to play them."

Clerk: "It can be fixed. You'll have to send it to the manufacturer's repair facility in Mahwah."

Customer: "I just bought it two days ago. I need it for a party tomorrow."

Clerk: "We can rent you a VCR for $30 a night."

Customer: "I spent $300 for a "good" VCR. I am entitled to a refund or a new one."

Clerk: "I am sorry. I can't help you."

Customer: "I would like to speak to the manager, please."

Manager: "I understand we have a problem

here.**99**

Customer: **66**I bought a VCR two days ago. It doesn't work. I want a new one or my money back.**99**

Manager: **66**We'll give you a free loaner while your machine is being repaired.**99**

Customer: **66**Would you deliver it to me? I live ten miles away.**99**

Manager: **66**Fine.**99**

✎ Conclusion

These conversations are typical. Millions of products are returned every month. If you have products that you are not satisfied with, organize yourself, write notes, bring a friend, and don't forget to **TAKE IT BACK!**

6

Warranties and Defective Products

This chapter was written by Joel D. Joseph, a Washington, D.C. attorney who specializes in consumer's rights.

Every product you buy comes with a warranty. There is only one exception to this, when you buy a product on an "as is" basis. There are two kinds of warranties: written and implied. Most home appliances, like blenders or toasters, come with written warranties. Clothing usually does not come with a written warranty, but all clothing comes with an implied warranty. This implied warranty means that a shirt will wear for a reasonable period of time, that it will not shrink excessively and it will not bleed.

☞ The Case of the Bleeding Shirt

I bought a very expensive designer shirt at Saks Fifth Avenue. The first time that I picked it up from the dry cleaners it was a disaster: my favorite shirt had been ruined! The formerly black and white plaid shirt had become a black and grey plaid shirt. The dry cleaner pleaded innocence, and sent the shirt to the International Fabricare Institute (800/638-2627) for testing.

The tests showed that the drycleaner was indeed innocent and that the shirt manufacturer had used defective dyes from a third-world country. The Institute sent the cleaners a scientific report of their results. Armed with this official report I marched into Saks Fifth Avenue and the clerk immediately took the shirt back and apologized.

☞ What Does an Implied Warranty Imply?

An implied warranty means that the product sold will do as it is supposed to do: a blender will blend, a lawnmower will cut grass, a typewriter will type and a computer will compute. It also means that the toy which you have to assemble will have all of the parts necessary for assembly. The offical legal term is that the product has an implied warranty of "fitness for intended use."

Getting back to the bleeding shirt, the implied warranty for a shirt is: a shirt is made to be washed or dry cleaned. It should not bleed or shrink after cleaning.

☞ How Long Should a Handbag Last?

The implied warranty also means that products should do what they are supposed to do for a reasonable amount of time. A friend of mine bought an expensive handbag from Macy's. She used the purse for six months when the catch for closing the bag broke. She took it back to the store and was told by a clerk that the handbag could not be repaired.

When the clerk was not helpful she asked to see the manager. The manager listened and examined the handbag. The manager agreed that the handbag should have lasted longer and directed the sales clerk to make a full refund.

Legally speaking Macy's was not required to make a full refund for a purse that was used for six months. Obviously, the handbag was used for a period of time and that use is worth something. Some stores would have offered to give a credit for one-half of the price of the item purchased. Macy's manager went beyond what was required to make the customer a happy customer.

☞ Coming Up Short

A friend bought a pair of denim shorts at Bloomingdales. The first time that the shorts were worn a metal button on the shorts caused a rust stain on the shirt that she was wearing. She brought the shorts and the shirt to Bloomingdales fuming that "the shorts had ruined my favorite white t-shirt!" The shirt was not even purchased at Bloomies, but they took both the shirt and the shorts back. The implied warranty for clothing extends to damage that the defective clothing caused. Since the metal button caused rust damage the store was legally required to give cash or credit to the customer for the damage done. Most large stores will give credit for minor damage caused by their products.

☞ Services, Services

Services, as well as products, come equipped with implied warranties. If you have a car repair performed and it is not done properly, you can have them do it over or give you a refund. A friend used a cleaning service to clean her townhouse. Her venetian blinds had not been cleaned properly so I advised her to call the service to have them come out again. The service came out again and recleaned the blinds. Now both the cleaning service and the customer are pleased because the cleaning service has gained a faithful customer and the faithful customer has a clean house.

☞ When the Warranty is in Writing

I bought a video cassette recorder with a 90 day warranty. Just after the 90th day the VCR got indigestion and started chewing video tapes. I brought the tape player back to the store where it was purchased. The store checked out the machine and determined that the problem was caused by a defect in manufacturing and that they would replace the VCR without charge. The point is that even if your written warranty period is over you can still try to return a defective product.

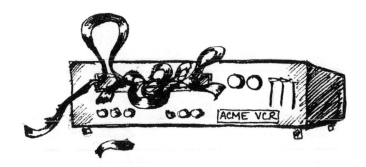

☞ Potentially Dangerous Products

Many years after owning a product you may learn that it poses an unnecessary hazard to you. For example, after years of use a toy may break apart exposing a sharp point, rough edge or other dangerous condition. The toy may have been recalled by the U.S. Consumer Product Safety Commission. To find out if a consumer product has been recalled by the CPSC you can call the CPSC Hotline at (800) 638-2772. The CPSC Hotline is a computerized service which responds to your touch-tone telephone. Various recorded messages on recalled products can be heard by dialing the hotline and then the following codes:

> 000 Directory of recalls
> 301 Toys
> 302 Indoor children's equipment and furniture
> 303 Outdoor children's equipment
> 304 Children's clothing
> 999 To file a complaint

The Consumer Product Safety Commission does not handle all product recalls. The Food and Drug Administration handles recalls of food, drugs and cosmetic products. The National Highway Traffic Safety Administration (HNTSA) is responsible for automobile safety and has jurisdiction over infant car seats. NHTSA can tell you if your car (or if a used car you are considering) has been recalled. NHTSA's auto safety hotline is calling (202) 366-0123.

☞ Repairs for Free after Warranty Expires

Manufacturers are very sensitive about bad publicity. Product safety is a matter of public concern and most manufacturers will repair an unsafe product even after the warranty period has expired. For example, I used to own a Volvo, whose manufacturer advertises its safety qualities. I had two safety-related defects on a four-year old car: the seatbelts did not work properly and the back-up lights went on when the car was going forward. The dealer would not do the work at no charge, so I wrote a letter to Volvo's United States headquarters explaining the problem and demanding a free repair. Volvo responded positively and the repairs were made without charge.

New cars are required to meet auto emission standards for 50,000 miles. That is the life expectancy for the car's primary pollution control device, the catalytic converter. Many cars with less than 50,000 miles on them start to belch black fumes, either due to a faulty catalytic converter or due to the need for an expensive valve job. If you have a fairly new car which has failed an emission test **TAKE IT BACK** to the car dealer. If they fail to repair the car without charge, read Chapter Eight of this book for advice on dealing with your lemon.

7

When They Won't Take It Back

Everyone has problems with consumer products and services. However, most of these problems are minor—the quality of the produce was poor, or the dishwasher repair man kept you waiting all day. For these types of problems your first course of action should be to take the product back, or to complain to the manager for the injustice. If you sued someone in small claims court for every minor consumer transgression, you could spend your life there.

It is necessary to divide the minor problems from the major ones—not always an easy task because the principles involved are usually more important than the dollar value of the problem. Some problems should be considered major even when the loss taken is relatively small. A toy which has little retail value, can become a major problem if it is dangerous. This holds true for electronic items as well.

Once you have decided whether the problem is

minor or major, then you can choose an appropriate course of action. Many minor and major problems can be resolved by speaking with the manager of the store where the product was purchased. If the manager is not helpful, or will not take the product back, tell him or her that you will not shop at their store anymore, and then don't. Talk to the manger first, then when you start calling and writing, vengance can rightly be yours.

A woman I know received a baby stroller as a shower gift. Before giving it to her, her friends took it out if the box to assemble it. The stroller did not appeal to her, so she went to the discount store where it was purchased to exchange it for another style. The store would not accept the stroller in return without the original packaging, even the manager was adamant about this. In the end there was nothing she could do but pursue the dispute with the manu-facturer, or just keep it. Because her baby was due in just a few short weeks, she decided that this was a very minor issue, so she kept it.

It is possible to spend too much time and energy trying to return unwanted merchandise. If you run into problems such as my friend with the stroller experien-ced, you might make the same decision as she did. The important thing to remember is that it's your choice. If it is worthwhile to pursue a return by all means do so.

All right, here you are, speaking with the manager has not helped, you're stuck with a broken Barbie Doll, or worse, a pneumatic pony, not only have you lost money, but your wrath must be assuaged. Here's what you can do:

✍️ Write A Consumer Complaint Letter

If you are not satisfied with a consumer product, you should complain both to the retail store where you purchased it and to the manufacturer. The address of the manufacturer should be on the product or the package that it came in. If the address is not on the product, ask the retail store for the manufacturer's address.

Your letter should be typed, and you should enclose a copy of your receipt. Make a copy of the letter for your records and keep the original receipt. Include the serial number of the product if it has one, the date of purchase, and the store where it was bought. Then explain the problem you are experiencing and describe what you want (a refund, a new product, or whatever). A sample complaint letter follows, spelling all of these elements out. Make sure, at the end of your letter, you state when you expect a reply.

It is often effective to address your letter to the president of the store. A list of major retail company presidents is included in Appendix One. A good technique to use to get his or her special attention is to put a "c.c." (carbon copy) at the bottom of the letter showing that a copy of the letter was sent to a state or federal agency.

Sample Complaint Letter

Your Name
Your Address

John Smith, President
Smith Company
Address

RE: (Nature of complaint and product)

I purchased one of your _____ products on _____ (date)
and I am very unhappy with it because _____
_____. The serial
number of the product is _____, and it is a _____ model. I
made this purchase at your store located in _____. A
copy of my receipt is enclosed. I tried to bring it back to the store on
_____ (date) but Mrs. B. Jones, a store clerk, refused to do so
claiming that it looked like the product had been "abused." I have
never abused a product and I have been a loyal customer for ten
years.

Unfortunately, your product (or service) has not performed
satisfactorily (or the service was inadequate) because
_____. In order to
resolve this matter I want you to exchange the product for a new one
(or return my purchase price, or whatever you, the customer, want
done).

I am looking forward to your reply and to a resolution of this
problem. I will wait three weeks (or whatever time limit you want to
set) before taking other action to resolve this dispute. Contact me at
the above address or by telephone at _____.

Sincerely yours,

YOUR NAME

c.c.: Office of Consumer Protection

✍️ HELP! I've Received No Reply

If you get no response within a reasonable amount of time, or you get a negative response, what do you do next? You basically have six options (not necessarily in this order):

❶ Write to an action line or hot line;

❷ Write to the Better Business Bureau;

❸ Write to a consumer action panel;

❹ Write to a state or local consumer protection

❺ Write to a federal agency; or

❻ File a small claim lawsuit against the store or manufacturer.

Your seventh choice is to do nothing. You will have to weigh the alternatives and decide how much time and money you are willing to invest to correct the problem. My friend Adam bought a football at K-Mart. One year later, through no fault of his own, the football developed a leak. I of course, told him to return it, but he claimed too much time had passed (sounds like a wimpy wonder to me). Then I suggested he write to the manufacturer, and his response was: "It's not worth it, I've used it for a year and it wasn't expensive in the first place." He weighed his options and decided to do nothing. I think any of the six choices above would have worked better for him, he probably would have a new football.

✍️ Action Lines

Most major cities have action lines or hot lines at newspapers, or at radio or television stations. A list of the action lines is included in Appendix Two at page 116.

✍️ Better Business Bureaus

Your local Better Business Bureau may help you resolve your problem. However, not all companies are members of the bureau, and the bureau can do little to help you if the business is not a member. If your product was manufactured in another city, the local bureau will probably not be able to help you, but a consumer action panel may be able to. A list of Better Business Bureaus is included in Appendix Three.

✍️ Consumer Action Panels

Several major industries have established consumer action panels to help resolve consumer complaints. The automotive and major appliance panels are the most active. The Auto Consumer Action Panel will be discussed in Chapter Eight. Decisions made by the major appliance panel are binding on the manufacturer, but not on the consumer. Major appliances include air conditioners, refrigerators, freezers, micro-wave ovens, washers, dryers and dishwashers. To contact the major appliance consumer panel write:

Major Appliance Consumer Action Panel
20 N. Wacker Drive, Suite 1550
Chicago, IL 60606
(312) 9845858

If you have a problem with a major appliance you can fill out the complaint form shown at the beginning of this chapter and mail it to MACAP.

✍️ State/Local Consumer Protection Agencies

Every state government has an office to handle consumer complaints regarding products and services. A list of these state agencies is included in Appendix Four. Many cities and counties also have consumer protection offices. States and cities license or regulate many professionals and businesses, such as doctors, nurses, accountants, pharmacists, funeral directors, plumbers, electricians, auto repair shops, collection agencies and electronic repair shops. These licensing boards can help you resolve your dispute. The boards or licensing agencies often have the power to revoke licenses and permits, so they have a lot of clout when dealing with license holders.

Concerning disputes about lawyers, doctors and dentists, you can complain to your state bar association, medical association, or dental association.

✍ Making a Federal Case out of It

Three major federal agencies handle consumer problems. They are the Federal Trade Commission, the Food and Drug Administration and the Consumer Product Safety Commission. The U.S. Postal Services handles consumer complaints concerning mail fraud.

The Federal Trade Commission (FTC) has regional offices which receive complaints concerning warranties, and complaints of unfair or deceptive trade practices. The FTC does not process individual complaints, but if it notices a pattern of complaints against one company, it will take action on behalf of all consumers who have had similar problems. If you believe that an advertisement is false or misleading, the FTC is the appropriate agency to complain to.

The Federal Trade Commission also regulates the mail order industry. The FTC has ruled that you must receive merchandise when the seller says you will, or you are entitled to a refund. If a specific time for delivery is not mentioned, the seller must ship the item within 30 days after receiving the order. If the seller contacts you to explain the reason for the delay, you have a right to cancel. If you fail to respond, it means that you agree to the delay. When you prepay for an item and then cancel, the seller must mail a refund within seven business days. If the sale was on a credit card your account must be adjusted within one billing cycle. When a mail order business fails to comply with these rules, write to the Federal Trade Commission, Washington, DC 20580, or your local postmaster.

Make a copy of the mail order advertisement or brochure and send it to the postmaster or the FTC with your complaint letter.

The Food and Drug Administration (FDA) handles complaints concerning food, drug and cosmetic products. The FDA can order immediate recalls if a product is likely to cause injury or death. For example, the FDA and Johnson & Johnson ordered the recall of some Tylenol products when there was a series of contaminated Extra-Strength Tylenol bottles.

The Consumer Product Safety Commission (CPSC) handles complaints concerning consumer products that may be dangerous. The CPSC regulates the safety of toys, bicycles, lawnmowers, insulation, electrical products, and dozens of everyday items. One phone call from a concerned mother led to the recall of millions of dangerous toys that McDonald's was giving away. Call the CPSC tollfree hotline: (800) 638-8326 (Maryland residents call: (800) 492-8363 and residents of Alaska, Hawaii, Puerto Rico, and the Virgin Islands can dial (800) 638-8333.) The CPSC has the power to ban, recall or regulate all unsafe products.

The U.S. Postal Service should be contacted when you believe a business is using the mail for fraudulent purposes. Write to the postmaster in your area at this simple address: Postmaster, your city, state and zip code. Mail fraud is a felony and the postmaster will refer cases to the United States Attorney for criminal prosecution.

✍ Suing in Small Claims Court

Small claims courts offer relief to consumers and can award a maximum of $300 to $5000 depending on the state. Most state limits range from about $750 to $1000. Filing fees are low, the lowest being about $2 and the highest $15. In as little as two weeks, without hiring an attorney, you can have a trial set and receive judgment against a company.

After filing a small claims case, a company who has ignored your letters will soon respond to you. Usually, a corporation must hire an attorney to represent it, even in most small claims courts.

✍ Vindication

I can not imagine that after you have followed through on one or more of these channels, you would not be compensated for your loss in one way or another. If you do not receive financial compensation or some other amicable arrangement, at minimum you know that as a consumer you have done the responsible thing. Peace of mind is knowing that others might benefit from your complaint.

8

Lemon Aid: Taking Your Car Back

Next to your home, a car is usually your largest investment. With economy cars selling for $10,000, it is indeed frustrating when the darn vehicle doesn't work properly. Here is an outline of the steps that you can take when your car is a lemon. If you are interested in more details about this see the *Lemon Book*, by Ralph Nader and Clarence Ditlow, published by Moyer Bell in 1990. The book can be ordered by calling (800) 759-4100.

There are eleven different actions that can be taken to deal with your new, or fairly new, automobile which seems to be in the repair shop more often than it is in your garage. These steps can be pursued in any order:

Actions to Consider

1. Complain to the dealer;
2. Complain to manufacturer's zone or regional representatives;
3. Complain to the main headquarters of the manufacturer;
4. Return your lemon;
5. File a complaint with the Automotive Consumer Action Program (AUTOCAP);
6. Write to the Federal Trade Commission;
7. Refuse to pay car loan (in certain cases);
8. Write to National Highway Traffic Safety Administration;
9. Write to Environmental Protection Agency;
10. File a complaint with a state or local Consumer Protection Office;
11. File suit.

❖ The Dealer

First off, unless your car is a total disaster, you should give your dealer an opportunity to repair the car. If the needed repair work is covered by the manufacturer's warranty, the dealer should make the repair. Even if the warranty period has expired, the dealer may make the repair under a so-called "secret" warranty. A secret warranty is made when a manufacturer has had repeated problems with a particular component of the car. It is secret because dealers are told to charge for the repairs unless the customer complains. So, by all means, make a vocal complaint. If you suspect that other people are experiencing the same problem you can call or write one of the following consumer groups:

Center for Auto Safety
2001 S Street, NW
Suite 410
Washington, DC 20009
(202) 328-7700

Motor Voters
1350 Beverly Road, Suite 115-240
McLean, VA 22101
(703) 448-0002

Consumer Education & Protection Assoc.
6048 Ogontz Avenue
Philadelphia, PA 19141
(215) 424-1441

Consumer Action—San Francisco
116 New Montgomery, Suite 223
San Francisco, CA 94105
(415) 777-9635

You also can write to the Better Business Bureau, or to an action line. Addresses of Better Business and action lines appear in appendices two and three. Send copies of your complaint letter to as many of these organizations as you want; it might strike a nerve somewhere and provoke assistance.

While the dealer who sold you the car should be responsive to your complaints you can go to any dealer who sells the car that you own. A large dealer may have had more experience with your type of problem. Some dealers have better service departments than others; if you are unhappy with one dealer, try another.

❖ Manufacturer's Representatives

Every auto manufacturer has an internal system for handling consumer complaints. Auto dealers are supervised by regional or zone representatives of the manufacturers. A list of contacts in the automobile industry is included in Appendix Eight. Your dealer will give you the name of the zone representative who services it. The zone rep may handle your complaint by phone, or he or she may want to meet you at a dealership to inspect your car. A zone or regional representative has the power to authorize warranty repairs, even when the warranty has expired.

❖ Corporate Headquarters

Occasionally, writing to the president of an auto manufacturer gets results. But the standard route is to write to the customer relations office at the corporation's headquarters. A list of these offices is included in Appendix Eight. A sample complaint letter is included at the end of this chapter.

❖ Returning Your Lemon

If your problems are substantial, and you have been deprived of the use of your car for a long time, you may be able to take back your lemon for a refund or an exchange. Before returning your car, you should consult with an attorney. Returning a car is risky because you may still be liable for car payments while the dispute is being worked out. Taking your car back is a last resort that should only be attempted when your problems are insoluble. If your car is turned in, make sure that you offer the dealer the keys and title, remove your license plates and notify your lender and insurance company.

For more information on returning your car see the *Lemon Book*, mentioned in the beginning of this chapter.

❖ Autocaps

There are 32 regional automobile consumer action programs, or Autocaps, across the United States. Appendix Eight includes a list of these Autocaps. The Autocaps have a standard form for filing complaints. This form is included at the end of this chapter. Each Autocap has a panel half composed of industry representatives and half of consumer representatives, who will review your complaint. The panels make a decision within three to four weeks that is usually adhered to by the manufacturer or dealer, but is not binding on you. If you disagree with the decision of the Autocap panel, you can pursue other remedies, through agencies or in court.

❖ The Federal Trade Commission

The Federal Trade Commission (FTC) will investigate cases where warranties are not lived up to or where there have been false or misleading advertisements. The FTC usually will not resolve an individual complaint, but it will step in where a pattern of fraud or warranty violations develops. The FTC has regional offices in major cities and a national office in Washington. The national office has a warranty project. If you have a warranty problem write to:

> Warranty Project
> Bureau of Consumer Protection
> Federal Trade Commission
> Washington, DC 20580

Concerning false advertising or other fraudulent practices, write to a regional FTC office. A list of these offices is included in Appendix Five.

❖ When You Have the Right to Refuse Payment on Your Car Loan

When a car dealer arranges your car loan through an affiliated lender, legally you may be entitled to stop making car payments when there are serious problems with your vehicle. You have the right to stop making payments on your GM car when GMAC provided financing, your Ford product when Ford Motor Credit made your loan, or when Chrysler Credit lent you money for your Chrysler product. However, if your credit union or bank made the car loan directly to you, you must continue to make car payments, even when your car is a lemon through and through.

❖ National Highway Traffic Safety Administration

The National Highway Traffic Safety Administration (NHTSA) is the federal agency that is responsible for most automobile recalls. NHTSA provides a consumer hotline to receive safety-related automotive complaints. NHTSA's number and address is:

National Highway Safety Traffic Administration
Auto Safety Hotline, NEFII HL
400 7th Street, S.W.
Washington, DC 20590
(202) 426-0123

NHTSA keeps track of all auto recalls, so you can call them to determine whether your car was ever the subject of a recall. If you are buying a used car, you should call the hotline to find out if the car has been recalled, and what it has been recalled for. NHTSA will need the car's vehicle identification number, make, model and year.

Safety-related defects cover a wide range of automotive problems. For example, excessive rusting can lead to safety problems and has been the subject of recalls. Stalling, and failing brakes, seatbelts, defrosters, turn signals or headlights, and many other problems have been investigated by NHTSA. If your car is recalled because of an order made by the traffic safety administration, the repairs will be paid for by the manufacturer, even if your warranty expired long ago. At the end of this chapter is an NHTSA questionnaire that informs the agency of safety-related problems.

❖ The Environmental Protection Agency

The Environmental Protection Agency can help you resolve auto complaints that at first glance, do not appear to concern the environment. For example, if your car, with 40,000 miles on it, needs a valve job because it is burning oil, the EPA may be able to get the work done at no cost to you, even though your warranty has expired. The Clean Air laws require all cars to meet emission requirements for five years or 50,000 miles. A car that burns oil in excess probably cannot meet the emission limits. Even if you bought the car used, the EPA can still help. If your car is smoking excessively or burning too much oil, or your catalytic converter does not work anymore, write the EPA a letter. To confirm that your car fails to comply with the air quality laws, you should get it inspected at your state's inspection service (if your state has an inspection program) or at a private inspection service. The address to send your complaint to is:

> Director
> Mobile Source Enforcement
> Environmental Protection Agency
> Washington, DC 20460

❖ Consumer Protection Agencies

Every state has an office to handle consumer complaints. If you have failed elsewhere, your state office may help you. A list of consumer protection agencies in each state is in Appendix Four. A massive case against General Motors began in Illinois when a consumer complained that his Oldsmobile had a Chevy engine in it. The Attorney General of Illinois filed a class action suit against GM, which was settled quickly. Each Oldsmobile owner who received a Chevy engine also received a check from General Motors to compensate for the switch. GM now informs consumers that the engine in its cars may have been manufactured by other GM divisions, and that your Cadillac may have a Buick engine. It only takes one irate consumer to make a difference.

❖ Taking Legal Action

If all else has failed, you should bring all your repair records and other documents to a lawyer. A half hour consultation should be worthwhile. The lawyer may convince you that you do not have a case, or may think the case is so good that he or she will represent you on a contingency fee basis. A contingency fee means the lawyer only gets paid if there is a victory. If there is a warranty related problem, the Magnuson–Moss Warranty Act provides that if you win the case the auto company must pay for the lawyer's fees, court costs and damages. The Center for Auto Safety or your local Bar Association may supply you with the names of a few lawyers who can represent you. If there is a small amount at stake, less than $1000, you may want to file a small claim against the dealer and the manufacturer.

Letter to Auto Manufacturer

Name
Address
City, State

Consumer Affairs Office
Automobile Manufacturer

RE: Vehicle Identification number
Model, year
Dealer Purchased from

Dear _____ ,

I purchased the above-described automobile on _____ (date) and have brought it back to the dealer _____ times to correct the same problems. I have lost _____ days from work in order to have the car repaired. My salary is $_____ per day; I have therefore lost $_____ in time lost from work. In addition I have had to rent a car for $_____ per day for _____ days, or a total of $_____ .

Enclosed are copies of repair bills and work orders to confirm these problems.

I want you to replace the car with a new one, or refund my purchase price of $_____ , or pay me $_____ for the damages that I have suffered. I expect your reply by _____ (date). If I do not have a satisfactory response from you by then, I will seek relief from a court or agency with jurisdiction over the matter.

Sincerely yours,

(Signature)

cc: Center for Auto Safety
Action Line

AUTOCAP Complaint Form

AUTOMOTIVE TRADE ASSOCIATION
NATIONAL CAPITAL AREA
15873 Crabbs Branch Way
Rockville, Maryland 20855
(301) 670-1110

Summary of Consumer Complaint

(Note: Before filling out this form, have you given the dealer an opportunity to respond to your problem? If not, we suggest that you contact the appropriate departmental manager "i.e., service manager, sales manager, whatever". You may find the matter can be resolved without a third party.)

Please print clearly or type. As we are particularly interested in the current status of your problem, please be brief and to the point, leaving out any irrelevant history. Do not make any reference to anyone's honesty or integrity as a copy of this statement will be sent to the company(s) involved.

Name: _____ Date: _____

Address: _____

Daytime Telephone: _____

Dealership Involved: _____

Name(s) of Dealer Representative dealt with (if known):

_____

Purchased: New   Used   Demo   From: _____

On (Date): _____ Current Mileage: _____

Is the Manufacturer Involved? _____ Which One? _____

Manufacturer's Representative(s) Involved:

_____

Are Any Other Agencies Involved? Yes No Which One(s)?

_____

Where Did You Hear About Autocap? _____

This problem concerns (circle appropriate numbers and letters).

1) Repairs	A) New Car Warranty	D) Financing
2) New Car Sales	B) Used Car Warranty	E) Service Guarantee
3) Used Car Sales	C) Purchase Agreement	F) Shop Charges
4) Demo Sale		

  1. Name parties and include dates (with vehicle mileage everywhere applicable).
    2. Note any action or offers by the dealer or manufacturer.
    3. Note what it is you are seeking.

  Attach copies of all supporting documents such as repair orders, purchase agreements, etc. Original documents are not required and this office assumes no responsibility for returning originals. Limit additional description to one other sheet.

_____
                                    SIGNATURE

OFFICE USE
Case #   Staff Member Handling Case

9

Return Policies

To understand the different return policies stores may have, first learn the four components of returns. These four major variables are:

① **Time period** for an acceptable return;

② Whether you need a **receipt**;

③ Acceptable **reasons** for a return;

④ Whether you will receive a **refund or credit**.

▥➡ Beat the Clock

Prompt returns are recommended by virtually all stores, though most will accept a return "within a reasonable period of time." What is a reasonable amount of time depends, of course, on the expected life span the item purchased. Compare for example, a quart of milk versus a vacuum cleaner. A reasonable time for one may be a week; the other a year or more. Seasonal items should be returned before the end of the season so that they can be resold.

Some stores have no time limit on returns. These are the stores to shop at.

⟩ Proof of Purchase

When you go to return an item, remember to bring your sales receipt with you. Receipts are encouraged by all stores, some even require them. Stores that don't require a receipt will often give you a speedier, more hassle-free return if you have one. Others, particularly mail-order houses, encourage customers to return merchandise in the original packaging along with the preprinted return form and return label.

➡ Reasons for the Return

Some stores will accept a return for any reason. Others require that the purchased item be defective in some way. In Chapter Three we suggested many possible reasons for wanting to return an item. Obviously, stores catering to customers will accept just about any reason, while others may give you the third degree before accepting a return.

➡ Cash or Charge?

When you paid cash for an item you are returning, it is very frustrating to be told you can only get store credit in return. This is especially true if the store is one you shop at infrequently. I recommend using credit cards to avoid this problem. Some stores, however, may refuse to even credit back your charge account, issuing store merchandise credit only. This practice is, frankly, outrageous and you should not stand for it.

Writing a check can result in an even greater hassle since, even if a store is willing to refund your purchase, they may require you to wait 10 days for your check to clear.

⏵ When Your Salesman is a Doubting Thomas

Knowing and understanding return policies is one thing, but sometimes making the salesperson accept the return is another. Over and over again, I have stressed how important it is to deal with the manager, and I have suggested various recourses if the manager doesn't listen. If you know for a fact that an employee is acting in direct violation of a store policy, by all means go straight to the top. Be polite, but refuse to leave the store if you have to. Make people listen to you, stand up for yourself. I am a conscientious shopper, but even I run into problems in stores. These are the stores I never go back to.

⏵ The Nordstrom Factor

Some nationally-known stores are moving toward more liberal return policies, allowing virtually unlimited time for returns. While this is good news for the consumer, you may wonder how even the largest stores can afford to accept returns on old merchandise. The fact is, such liberal return policies do cost the big stores money. It is worth it for them only because such policies have proven they build customer loyalty. These stores have determined that loyal customers are worth the cost of the liberal return policies. One of the first stores to adopt this policy, and the store to do it most successfully, is Nordstrom.

Throughout its ninety years of operations and three generations of family leadership, one thing has remained at Nordstrom: its strict customer focus. Ask any Nordstrom sales person what the company's philosophy is, and he or she will tell you, "customer service."

Nordstrom's strategy is to pamper its customers, no matter how small a purchase they make, through personal service, extensive selections and lenient return policies. Stories of the extraordinary efforts of Nordstrom and its sales staff and management are legion. My favorite story appeared on a 1989 CBS Morning News segment focused on service-oriented companies. The reporter humorously relayed that because some Nordstrom customers have been known to return nylon hose after developing runs due to wear, Nordstrom has been dubbed the "Rent-a-hose" store.

Another famous Nordstrom return story involves a man who wanted to return a pair of tires. Nordstrom does not, and never has carried tires in any of its stores. Nonetheless, the sales clerk gladly took the tires back.

We wrote to Norstrom and asked them to tell us why they have such a liberal return policy. Jack McMillan, Nordstrom's president replied, "our return policy, which is the cornerstone of our customer service policy, is to pretty much give the customer what they want. In essence, we ask our salespeople not to say 'no' to the customer. This seems to satisfy their needs, and they keep on coming back."

Obviously, this strategy of catering to the customer has paid off for Nordstrom, which has enjoyed phenomenal success. What's more, stores that have not been as customer-service oriented have been losing business to Norstrom, which has the most loyal customers in the business. Other retailers are scrambling to emulate the Nordstrom success factor of catering to the customer, thereby benefitting all consumers.

➠ Beware of Boutiques

Usually the worst return policies come from the small boutique retailers. In these often posh establishments a small discreet sign will state "Merchandise Must Be Returned Within Seven Days." Many of these time restrictions are iron-clad rules, these stores cater to impulse buying, not impusle returning. Boutiques also will give only store credit rather than a refund.

➡ Discounters

Some stores that offer marked-down merchandise have tough return policies. For example, Syms offers excellent prices on quality clothing. However Syms will not make a refund, but only store credit for returns. You must keep these store policies in mind when shopping. A bargain may not be a bargain if you can't return it, and the store does not have something else that you need.

➡ National Chains

National stores usually have the most liberal return policies. Sears, for example, advertises that it will return anything bought at any branch of the chain. Sears' Craftsman hand tools come with a lifetime warranty: they may be exchanged years later if the tool breaks.

⮕ Mailorder Miscues

Ordering products by mail can save gasoline and time, but often products opened with anticipation are disappointing. Colors often look brighter or deeper in catalogues than they do in your living room, and as every shopper knows, a size eight skirt sometimes seems more like a six or a 10, depending on the manufacturer. For these reasons the return policies of major mail order houses, like Spiegel and L.L. Bean, are specially designed to make returns easy and thus appeal to consumers.

⮕ Returnability is a Service

Return policies are one of the services that you buy when you shop at a certain store. You have a right to know what a store policy is upfront, and every employee should be able to tell you the same answer. If the return policy is not posted ask "What is your return policy?" By knowing what to expect when you shop, you can avoid unnecessary hassles later, and in addition, make sure that you are receiving a fair deal.

10

Making a List and Checking it Twice

A Call to Action

Getting and giving a fair deal is a main ethic upon which this country was built. What would have happened if the British had not charged such a high tax on tea? We might not have a country. The Founding Fathers envisioned the United States as a nation in which injustice would always be met with rebellion and resistance, in which the people had the right to make changes in the system to better their lives.

As in any system, this challenge works both ways. As a seller, in order to make good, you must give a good deal, but in order to give a good deal you have to know what your buyer wants. How can you the consumer expect a good deal, if you are not communicating to the seller what a good deal is?

As it stands now, the retail chain-of-events in our society goes something like this: a) you the consumer are informed by very sophisticated advertising that you need product X to maintain or improve the quality of your life; b) you buy product X and find that it does or does not live up to your expectations; c) if X does do as it said it would you are a happy consumer, and you buy more of X; d) if X does not perform as expected, according to my research, you consume it, use it, wear it or keep it anyway, your expectations go down, and you might even buy X again. Something is wrong with this picture!

Over the course of chapters one through nine, I have tried to show you what a fair shake is, and what to do if you are not receiving proper treatment. I have offered suggestions on how to prepare for a happy return, and how to avoid hateful sellers and hassles. I have pointed out what you're responsibilities as a consumer are, and how to assure you are exercising your rights. Now I am offering you a call to action: if you don't like it, or you don't want it—**TAKE IT BACK!**

You know who you are—the consumer, and you know you have the right to be satisfied with a product, and get your money's worth from a service. If you're not happy somebody is going to have to do something, because you're not going to take **NO** for an answer. If every consumer stood up for their rights the way you do, no one would ever get gypped, duped or ripped-off again. We're sick of shoddy goods made god-knows-where, and we're not going to keep them anymore! We're tired of sleepy people telling us what we can and cannot do, if our car is in the shop we're not going to rent a car, you're going to rent it for us!

You not only have the power to change your wimpy ways, but you have the power to change the face of retail for others less fortunate than you, who don't know their shopper's rights. If Nordstom can force competitors towards more lenient return policies, so can you.

✎ Return Checklist

Now that you can recognize good shopping and returning techniques, and you know how to use them, all your excuses for backing out of that essential return have dissappeared with the ill-tempered north wind. With your cheeriest face on, packages in hand, you set out for the mall. With great expectations you are even looking forward to this return, because you have made this list (if you need to) and checked it twice, and you know it's going to be hassle-free, smooth sailing, a hot knife through butter, and your little red wagon is going to squeek no more!

Many
Happy
Returns

Always! Always! Always!

☐ Return mechandise in good condition;

☐ Bring your receipt, or credit card statement;

☐ Know your reasons;

☐ Be firm and confident;

☐ Don't feel guilty;

☐ Be prepared to compromise;

☐ Ask for the manager if you run into trouble;

☐ DON'T TAKE NO FOR AN ANSWER!

The form on the next page may be helpful for people who have a difficult time organizing themselves, or for those who have trouble staying cool and clear in confrontational situations, I believe it contains everything anyone would need to know. It can also help you monitor in the short term the status of a return, and in the long term your overall success in your new life as an assertive shopper. It may surprise you just how much stuff you don't want or need when you have the option to **TAKE IT BACK!**

Good luck and happy returns!

Checklist - Return Plan

Item to be returned: _____

Where purchased: _____

Date purchased: _____ Amount paid: $_____

Purchased by: _____

If gift, date received:_____ From: _____

Have receipt? Yes   No

Method of payment: Cash   Check   Charge

Reason(s) for Return (Check all that apply)

☐ 1. Doesn't fit properly

☐ 2. Faded or bled

☐ 3. Color wrong or did not coordinate

☐ 4. Defective

☐ 5. Arrived too late

☐ 6. Parts missing

☐ 7. Returning a gift

☐ 8. Changed mind; don't like it

☐ 9. Ordered two or more, returning one

☐10. Found a lower price

☐11. Other

_____

_____

_____

_____

_____

_____

_____

Date returned: _____

Outcome: _____

Notes:

_____

_____

_____

Checklist - Return Plan

Item to be returned: _____

Where purchased: _____

Date purchased: _____ Amount paid: $_____

Purchased by: _____

If gift, date received:_____ From: _____

Have receipt?   Yes   No

Method of payment: Cash   Check   Charge

Reason(s) for Return (Check all that apply)

☐ 1. Doesn't fit properly

☐ 2. Faded or bled

☐ 3. Color wrong or did not coordinate

☐ 4. Defective

☐ 5. Arrived too late

☐ 6. Parts missing

☐ 7. Returning a gift

☐ 8. Changed mind; don't like it

☐ 9. Ordered two or more, returning one

☐10. Found a lower price

☐11. Other

_____

_____

_____

_____

_____

_____

Date returned: _____

Outcome: _____

Notes:

_____

_____

_____

Checklist - Return Plan

Item to be returned: _____

Where purchased: _____

Date purchased: _____ Amount paid: $_____

Purchased by: _____

If gift, date received:_____ From: _____

Have receipt?   Yes   No

Method of payment: Cash   Check   Charge

Reason(s) for Return (Check all that apply)

☐ 1. Doesn't fit properly

☐ 2. Faded or bled

☐ 3. Color wrong or did not coordinate

☐ 4. Defective

☐ 5. Arrived too late

☐ 6. Parts missing

☐ 7. Returning a gift

☐ 8. Changed mind; don't like it

☐ 9. Ordered two or more, returning one

☐10. Found a lower price

☐11. Other

_____

_____

_____

_____

_____

_____

Date returned: _____

Outcome: _____

Notes:

_____

_____

_____

Appendix One

Mailing Addresses of Presidents

of Major Retail Stores

Jeffrey Sherman
President
Bloomingdales
132 W.31st St.
New York, NY 10001

Steve Watson
President
Dayton/Hudson (also Marshall Fields)
777 Nicolet Mall
Minneapolis, MN 55402

Sam Simmons
President
Jordan Marsh
450 Washington St.
Boston, MA 02205

Mr. Antoninni
President
K-Mart
3100 West Big Bear Road
Troy, MI 48084

Verna Gibson
President
The Limited
P.O. Box 16555
Columbus, OH 43272

Michael J. Vastola
President
Lionel Kiddie City
961 Grant Ave
Philadelphia, Pa. 19114

Herbert Yalof
President
Macys
151 W. 34th St.
New York, NY 10001

Rosemarie Bravo
Chairman
I. Magnin
Union Sq.
San Francisco, CA 94108

Ken Fokol
President
The May Company (and Hecht Co.)
6106 Laurel Canyon Blvd.
North Hollywood, CA 91606

Bernard Brennan
President
Montgomery Ward
44 Larrabee
Chicago, IL 60610

Terry Lundgren
President
Nieman-Marcus
Main and Ervay Streets
Dallas, TX 75201

Jack McMillan
President
Nordstrom
1501 5th Ave
Seattle, WA 48101

William Howe
President
J.C. Penney
PO Box 659000
Dallas, TX 75265

Roger Farah
President
Rich's Department Store
45 Broad St.
Atlanta, GA 30302

Joel J. Mathews
President
Saks Fifth Avenue
611 5th Avenue
New York, NY 10022

Customer Relations
Sears, BSD39-32
Sears Tower
Chicago, IL 60684

John Shea
President
Spiegel Catalog
1040 W. 35th St
Chicago, IL 60667

Sy Syms
President
Syms
1 Syms Way
Secaucus, NJ 07094

Charles Lazarus
President
Toys R Us
461 From Road
Paramus, NJ 07652

Sam Walton
President
Wal-Mart
702 S.W. 8th St.
Bentonville, AR 72716

Mickey Drexler
President
The Gap
900 Cherry Ave.
San Bruno, CA 94066

Appendix Two

Call for Action Affiliates

District of Columbia

WTOP Call for Action
4646 40th Street, N.W.
Washington, DC 20016
(202) 686-8225
11 a.m.-1 p.m.

Florida

WCIX-TV CFA
1111 Brickell Avenue
Miami. FL 33131
(305) 371-6566
11 a.m.-1 p.m.

Illinois

WIND CFA
625 N. Michigan Avenue
Chicago, IL 60611
(312) 644-0560
11 a.m.-1 p.m.

Indiana

WOWO CFA
203 W. Wayne Street
Ft. Wayne, IN 46802
(219) 424-2400

Kansas

KCMO-TV CFA
4500 Johnson Drive
Fairway, KS 66205
(913) 677-7381
11 a.m.-1 p.m.

Maryland

WBAL CFA
3800 Hooper Street
Baltimore, M D 21211
(301) 366-5900
11 a.m.-1 p.m.

Massachusetts

WBZ CFA
1170 Soldiers Field Road
Boston, MA 02134
(617) 787-2300
11 a.m.-1 p.m.

WBSM CFA
P.O. Box J4105
New Bedford, MA 02741
(617) 997-3349
11 a.m.-1 p.m.

Michigan

WJR CFA
Fisher Building
Detroit, Ml 48202
(313) 873-8700
11 a.m.-l p.m.

Missouri

KMOX CFA
One Memorial Drive
St. Louis, MO 63102
(314) 421-1975
11 a.m.-l p.m.

New York

WIVB-TV CFA
2077 Elmwood Avenue
Buffalo, NY 14207
(716) 874-1700
10 a.m.-12 noon

WGSM CFA
900 Walt Whitman Road
Huntington, NY 11747
(516) 423-1400

WMCA CFA
888 Seventh Avenue
New York, NY 10019
(212) 586-6666
11 a.m.-l p.m.

WGY CFA
1400 Balltown Road
Schenectady, NY 12309

(518) 385-1488
11 a.m.-l p.m.

WHEN CFA
P.O. Box 6509
Syracuse, NY 13217
(315) 467-6116
11 a.m.-l p.m.

North Carolina

WRAL-TV CFA
115 E. Chapel Hill Street
Durham, NC 27701
(919) 688-9306
11 a.m.-l p.m.

WRAL-TV CFA
209 S. McDowell Street
Raleigh, NC 27601
(919) 832-7578
11 a.m.-l p.m.

Ohio

WJKW-TV CFA
5800 Marginal Road
Cleveland, OH 44103
(216) 5780700
10 a.m.-12 noon

WFMJ CFA
101 W. Boardman
Youngstown, OH 44503
(216) 744-5155
11 a.m.-l p.m.

Pennsylvania

WFBG CFA
Logan Valley Boulevard
Altoona, PA 16603
(814) 944-9336
1 p.m.-3 p.m.
7 p.m.-9 p.m. Th

KYW CFA
5th S. Market Street
Philadelphia, PA 19106
(215) 925-1060
11 a.m.-1 p.m.

KDKA CFA
One Gateway Center
Pittsburgh, PA 15222
(412) 333-937
11 a.m.-1 p.m.

Tennessee

WDIA CFA
P.O. Box 12045
Memphis, TN 38112
(901) 278-6316
11 a.m.-1 p.m.

Appendix Three

Better Business Bureaus

California

705 Eighteenth Street
Bakersfield, CA 93301
(805) 322-2074

1265 North La Cadena
Colton, CA 92324
(714) 825-7280

413 Patterson Building
Fresno, CA 93721
(209) 268-6424

639 S. New Hampshire Ave.
3rd Floor
Los Angeles, CA 90005
(213) 383-0992

360 22nd Street, El Dorado Building
Oakland, CA 94612
(415) 839-5900

742731/2 Highway 111
Palm Desert, CA 92260
(714) 346-2014

1401 21st Street
Suite 305
Sacramento, CA 95814
(916) 443-6843

4310 Orange Avenue
San Diego, CA 92105
(714) 283-3927

2740 Van Ness Avenue
Suite 210
San Francisco, CA 94109
(415) 775-3300

P.O. Box 8110
San Jose, CA 95155
(408) 298-5880

20 North San Mateo Drive
P.O. Box 294
San Mateo, CA 94401
(415) 347-1251

P.O. Box 746
Santa Barbara, CA 93102
(805) 963-8657

111 North Center Street
Stockton, CA 95202
(209) 948-4880

17662 Irvine Boulevard
Suite 15
Tustin, CA 92680
Inquiries (714) 544-5842
Complaints 544-6942

Colorado

524 South Cascade
Col. Springs, CO 80903
(303) 636-1155

841 Delaware Street
Denver, CO 80204
(303) 629-1036

Connecticut

Fairfield Woods Plaza
2345 Black Rock Turnpike
Fairfield, CT 06430
(203) 368-6538

250 Constitution Plaza
Hartford, CT 06103
(203) 247-8700

35 Elm Street
P.O. Box 2015
New Haven, CT 06506
(203) 787-5788

Delaware

20 South Walnut St.
P.O. Box 300
Milford, DE 19963
(302) 856-6969

1901B West 11th St.
P.O. Box 4085
Wilmington, DE 19807
(302) 652-3833

District of Columbia

1334 G Street, N.W.
Prudential Building
6th Floor
Washington, DC 20005
(202) 393-8000

Florida

8600 NE 2nd Avenue
Miami, FL 33138
(305) 757-3446

3015 Exchange Court
W. Palm Beach, FL 33409
(305) 686-2200

Georgia

212 Healey Bldg.
57 Forsyth St. N.W.
Atlanta, GA 30335
(404) 688-4910

P.O. Box 2085
Augusta, GA 30903
(404) 722-1574

Martin Theatre Bldg.
1320 Broadway
Suite 250
Columbus, GA 31902
(404) 324-0712

P.O. Box 13956
Savannah, GA 31406
(912) 234-5336

Hawaii

677 Ala Moana Blvd.
Suite 602
Honolulu, HI 96813
(808) 531-8131

P.O. Box 11414
Lahaina, Maui, HI 96761
(808) 877-4000

Idaho

Idaho Building
Suite 324
Boise, ID 83702
(208) 342-4649

Illinois

35 East Wacker Drive
Chicago, IL 60601
Inquiries (312) 346-3868
Complaints 346-3313

109 S.W. Jefferson St.
Suite 305
Peoria, IL 61602
(309) 673-5194

Indiana

118 S. Second Street
P.O. Box 405
Elkhart, IN 46515
(219) 293-5731

Old Courthouse Center

Room 310
Evansville, IN 47708
(812) 422-6879

1203 Webster Street
Fort Wayne, IN 46802
(219) 423-4433

2500 West Ridge Road
Calumet Township
Gary, IN 46408
(219) 980-1511

15 East Market Street
Indianapolis, IN 46204
(317) 637-0197

204 Iroquois Building
Marion, IN 46952
(317) 668-8954

Ball State Univ. BBB
Whitinger Building
Room 160
Muncie, IN 47306
(317) 285-6375

230 West Jefferson Blvd.
South Bend, IN 46601
(219) 234-0183

105 S. Third Street
Terre Haute, IN 47801
(812) 234-7749

Iowa

619 Kahl Building
Davenport, IA 52801
(319) 322-0782

234 Insurance Exch. Bldg.
Des Moines, IA 50309
(515) 243-8137

Benson Building
Suite 645
7th & Douglas Streets
Sioux City, IA 51101
(712) 252-4501

Kansas

501 Jefferson
Suite 24
Topeka, KS 66607
(913) 232-0454

300 Kaufman Building
Wichita, KS 67202
(316) 263-3146

Kentucky

1523 North Limestone
Lexington, KY 40505
(606) 252-4492

844 S. Fourth Street
Louisville, KY 40202
(502) 583-6546

Louisiana

2055 Wooddale Blvd.
Baton Rouge, LS 70806
(504) 926-3010

300 Bond Street
P.O. Box 9129
Houma, LA 70361
(504) 868-3456

804 Jefferson Street
P.O. Box 3651
Lafayette, LA 70502
(318) 234-8341

1413 Ryan Street, Suite C
P.O. Box 1681
Lake Charles, LA 70602
(318) 433-1633

141 De Siard Street
Suite 503
Monroe, LA 71201
(318) 387-4600

301 Camp Street
Suite 403
New Orleans, LA 70130
(504) 5816222

320 Milam Street
Shreveport, LA 71101
(318) 221 8352
(Texarkana residents call
(214) 7927691)

Maryland

401 North Howard Street
Baltimore, MD 21201
(301) 6856986

Montgomery County
(301) 309-0500

Massachusetts

8 Winter Street
Boston, MA 02108
(617) 4829151

The Federal Building
Suite 1
78 North Street
Hyannis, MA 02601
(617) 771-3022

316 Essex Street
Lawrence, MA 01840
(617) 687-7666

908 Purchase Street
New Bedford, MA 02745
(617) 999-6060

293 Bridge Street
Suite 324
Springfield, MA 01103
(413) 734-3114

32 Franklin Street
P.O. Box 379
Worcester, MA 01601
(617) 755-2548

Michigan

150 Michigan Avenue
Detroit, Ml 48226
(313) 962-7566

1 Peoples Building
Grand Rapids, MI 49503
(616) 774-8236
Holland/ Zeeland
(616) 772-6063

Muskegon
(616) 722-0707

Minnesota

1745 University Avenue
St. Paul, MN 55104
(612) 646-4637

Mississippi

P.O. Box 2090
Jackson, MS 39205
(601) 948-4732

Missouri

906 Grand Avenue
Kansas City, MO 64106
(816) 421-7800

Mansion House Center
440 N. Fourth Street
St. Louis, MO 63101
(314) 241-3100

P.O. Box 4331, GS 319
Hollard Building
Springfield, MO 65806
(417) 862-9231

Nebraska

719 North 48th Street
Lincoln, NE 68504
(402) 467-5261

417 Farnam Building
1613 Farnam Street
Omaha, NE 68102
(402) 346-3033

Nevada

1829 East Charleston Blvd.
Suite 103
Las Vegas, NV 89104
(702) 382-7141

372A Casazza Drive
P.O. Box 2932
Reno, NV 89505
(702) 322-0657

New Hampshire
One Pillsbury Street
Concord, NH 03301
(603) 224-1991

New Jersey
836 Haddon Avenue
P.O. Box 303
Collingswood, NJ 08108
(609) 854-8467

Mercer County
Cranbury, NJ 08512
(609) 586-1464

Monmouth County
536-6306

Middlesex, Somerset and
Hunderton Counties
297-5000

34 Park Place
Newark, NJ 07102
(201) 643-3025

2 Forest Avenue
Paramus, NJ 07652
(201) 845-4044

1721 Route 37 East
Toms River, NJ 06753
(201) 270-5577

New Mexico

2921 Carlisle, N.E.
Albuquerque, NM 87110
(505) 844-0500

2120 East 20th Street
Farmington, NM 87401
(505) 325-1136

Santa Fe Division
227 East Palace Avenue
Suite C
Santa Fe, NM 87501
(505) 988-3648

New York

775 Main Street
Buffalo, NY 14203
(716) 856-7180

435 Old Country Road
Westbury, NY 11590
(Long Island)
(516) 334-7662

257 Park Avenue, South
New York, NY 10010
Inquiries & Complaints
(212) 5336200
Other (212) 533-7500

257 Park Avenue, South
(Harlem)

New York, NY 10010
(212) 533-6200

1122 Sibley Tower
Rochester, NY 14604
(716) 546-6776

120 East Washington St.
Syracuse, NY 13202
(315) 479-6635

209 Elizabeth Street
Utica, NY 13501
(315) 724-3129

158 Westchester Avenue
White Plains, NY 10601
(914) 428-1230

120 East Main
Wappinger Falls, NY 12590
(914) 297-6550

North Carolina

291/2 Page Avenue
Asheville, NC 28801
(704) 253-2392

Commerce Center
Suite 1300
Charlotte, NC 28202
(704) 332-7152

3608 West Friendly Ave.
P.O. Box 2400
Greensboro, NC 27410
(919) 852-4240

100 Park Drive Building
Suite 203
P.O. Box 12033
Research Triangle, NC 27709
(919) 549-8221

First Union Nat. Bank Bldg.
Winston-Salem, NC 27101
(919) 725-8348

Ohio

P.O. Box F 596
Akron, OH 44308
(216) 253-4590

500 Cleveland Avenue, No.
Canton, OH 44702
(216) 454-9401

26 East Sixth Street
Cincinnati, OH 45202
(513) 421-3015

1720 Keith Building
Cleveland, OH 44115
(216) 241-7678

527 South High Street
Columbus, OH 43215
(614) 221-6336

15 East Fourth Street
Suite 209
Dayton, OH 45402
(513) 222-5825

405 N. Huron Street
Toledo, OH 45604
(419) 241-6276

903 Mahoning Bank Bldg.
P.O. Box 1495 44501
Youngstown, OH 44503
(216) 744-3111

Oklahoma

606 N. Dewey
Oklahoma City, OK 73102
(405) 239-6081, 82,83

4833 South Sheridan
Suite 412
Tulsa, OK 74145
(918) 664-1266

Oregon

623 Corbett Building
Portland, OR 97204
(503) 226-3981

Pennsylvania

528 North New Street
Dodson Building
Bethlehem, PA 18018
(215) 866-8780

53 N. Duke Street
Lancaster, PA 17602
Toll Free, York Co.
(717) 846-2700

1218 Chestnut Street
Philadelphia PA 19107
(215) 574-3600

610 Smithfield Street
Pittsburgh, PA 15222
(412) 456-2700

Brooks Building
Scranton, PA 18503
(717) 342-9129

Puerto Rico

P.O. Box BBB, Fernandez
Juncos Station
San Juan, PR 00910
(809) 724-7474

Rhode Island

248 Weybosset Street
Providence, RI 02903
(401) 272-9800

Tennessee

716 James Building
735 Broad Street
Chattanooga, TN 37402
(615) 266-6144

P.O. Box 3608
Knoxville, TN 37917
(615) 522-2139

1835 Union, Suite 202
P.O. Box 41406
Memphis, TN 38104
(901) 272-9641

Nashville City Bank Bldg.
Suite 506
Nashville, TN 37201
(615) 254-5872

Texas

465 Cypress Duffy Bldg.
P.O. Box 3275
Abilene, TX 79604
(915) 677-8071

518 Amarillo Building
Amarillo, TX 79101
(806) 374-3735

American Bank Tower
Suite 720
Austin, TX 78701
(512) 476-6943

P.O. Box 2988
Beaumont, TX 77704
(713) 835-5348

202 Varisco Bldg.
Bryan, TX 77801
(713) 823-8148

109 Chaparral
Suite 101
Corpus Christi, TX 78401
(512) 888-5555

1511 Bryan Street
Dallas, TX 75201
(214) 747-8891

2501 North Mesa Street
Suite 301
El Paso, TX 79902
(915) 533-2431

709 Sinclair Building
106 West 5th Street
Fort Worth, TX 76102
(817) 332-7585

P.O. Box 7499
Houston, TX 77008
(713) 868-9500

1015 15th Street
P.O. Box 1178
Lubbock, TX 79401
(806) 763-0459

Air Terminal Building
P.O. Box 6006
Midland, TX 79701
(915) 563-1880
Complaints 563-1882

337 West Twohig
San Angelo, TX 76903
(915) 653-2318

400 West Market Street
Suite 301
San Antonio, TX 78205
(512) 225-5833

608 New Road
P.O. Box 7203
Waco, TX 76718
(817) 772-7530

First National Bank Bldg.
Suite 600
Wichita Falls, TX 76301
(817) 723-5526

Utah

40 North 100 East
Provo, UT 84601
(801) 377-2611

1588 South Main
Salt Lake City, UT 84115
(801) 487-4656

Virginia

105 East Annandale Rd.
Suite 210
Falls Church, VA 22046
(703) 533-1900

First & Merchants Bldg.
Suite 620
300 Main Street, E.
P.O. Box 3548
Norfolk, VA 23514
(804) 627-5651

Peninsula area
(804) 851-9101

4020 West Broad St.
Richmond, VA 23230
(804) 355-7902

646 A Crystal Tower
145 West Campbell Ave. SW
Roanoke, VA 24011
(703) 342-3455

Appendix Four

State Consumer Protection Offices

Alabama

2026 Second Avenue N.
Suite 2303
Birmingham, AL 35203
(205) 323-6127

Central Bank Building
Suite 410
West Side Square
P.O. Box 383
Huntsville, AL 35801
(205) 533-1640

307 Van Antwerp Building
Mobile, AL 36602
(205) 433-5494

60 Commerce Street
Suite 810
Montgomery, AL 36104
(205) 262-2390

Consumer Protection Division
Office of Attorney General
560 South McDonough Street
Montgomery, AL 36104
(205) 832-5936
(809) 392-5658

Alaska

Consumer Protection Section
Office of Attorney General
1049 West Fifth Avenue
Suite 101
Anchorage, AK 99501
(907) 2790428

Arizona

4428 North 12th Street
Phoenix, AZ 85013
(602) 2641721

100 East Alameda Street
Suite 403
Tucson, AZ 84701
Inquiries (602) 622-7651
Complaints (602) 622-7654

Financial Fraud Division
Office of Attorney General
207 State Capitol Building
Phoenix, AZ 85007
(602) 255-5763
(800) 354-8431

Arkansas

Consumer Protection Division
Office of Attorney General
Justice Building
Little Rock, AR 72201

(501) 371-2341
(800) 482-8982

1216 South University
Little Rock, AR 72204
(501) 664-7274

California

California Department of
Consumer Affairs
1020 N Street
Sacramento, CA 95814
(916) 445-0660 (Complaint assistance)
(916) 445-1254 (Consumer information)

Colorado

AntiTrust and Consumer
Protection Section
Office of Attorney General
1525 Sherman Street
2nd Floor
Denver, CO 80203
(303) 866-3611

Connecticut

Department of Consumer Protection
State Office Building
165 Capitol Avenue

Hartford, CT 06115
(203) 566-4999
(800) 842-2649 (Connecticut only)

Delaware

Delaware Division of Consumer Aff
Department of Community Affairs
and Economic Development
820 North French Street
4th Floor
Wilmington, DE 19801
(302) 571-3250

District of Columbia

D.C. Office of Consumer Protection
1424 K Street, NW
2nd Floor
Washington, DC 20005
(202) 727-1158

Florida

Division of Consumer Services
110 Mayo Building
Tallahassee, FL 32301
(904) 488-2221
(800) 342-2176 (Florida only)

Georgia

Governor's Office of
Consumer Affairs
205 Butler Street, S.E.
Suite 356
Plaza Level East Tower
Atlanta, GA 30334

(404) 656-3790
(800) 282-4900

Hawaii

Governor's Office of
Consumer Protection
250 South King Street
P.O. Box 3767
Honolulu, HI 96812
(808) 548-2560

Idaho

Business Regulation Division
Office of Attorney General
State Capitol
Boise, ID 83720
(208) 334-2400

Illinois

Consumer Protection Division
Office of Attorney General
228 North LaSalle
Room 1242
Chicago, IL 60601
(312) 793-3580

Assistant Attorney General
Consumer Protection Division
Office of Attorney General
500 South Second Street
Springfield, IL 62706
(217) 782-9011

Indiana

Consumer Protection Division
Office of Attorney General
219 State House
Indianapolis, IN 46204
(317) 232-6330 or 6331
(800) 382-5516 (Indiana only)

Iowa

Assistant Attorney General
Consumer Protection Division
Office of Attorney General
1300 East Walnut
2nd Floor
Des Moines, IA 50319
(515) 281-5926

Kansas

Deputy Attorney General
Consumer Protection and
Antitrust Division
Office of Attorney General
Kansas Judicial Center
2nd Floor
Topeka, KS 66612
(913) 296-3751
(800) 432-2310

Kentucky

Assistant Deputy Attorney General
Consumer Protection Division Office
209 St. Clair Street
Frankfort, KY 40601
(502) 564-2200

(800) 432-9257 (Kentucky only)

Louisiana

State Office of Consumer Protection
2610A Wooddale Boulevard
P.O. Box 44091
Capitol Station Baton
Rouge, LA 70804
(504) 925-4401
(800) 272-9868

Maine

Bureau of Consumer Protection
Department of Business Regulation
State House Station No. 35
Augusta, ME 04333
(207) 289-3731

Maryland

Consumer Protection Division
Office of Attorney General
26 South Calvert Street
Baltimore, MD 21202
(301) 659-4300

Massachusetts

SelfHelp Consumer Information Office
Executive Office of Consumer Affairs
John W. McCormack Building
One Ashburton Place
Room 1411
Boston, MA 02108
(617) 727-7780

Michigan

Michigan Consumers Council
414 Hollister Building
106 West Allegan Street
Lansing, Ml 48933
(517) 373-0947
(800) 292-5680

Minnesota

Special Assistant Attorney General
Consumer Protection Division
Office of Attorney General
Room 200
117 University Avenue
St. Paul, MN 55155
(612) 296-3353

Mississippi

Consumer Protection Division
Department of Agriculture
High and President Streets
P.O. Box 1609
Jackson, MS 39205
(601) 354-6258

Missouri

Missouri Department of
Consumer Affairs
Regulation and Licensing
P.O. Box 1157
Jefferson City, MO 65102
(314) 751-4996

Montana

Consumers Affairs Unit
Department of Commerce
1424 Ninth Avenue
Helena, MT 59620
(406) 449-3163

Nevada

Consumer Affairs Division
Department of Commerce
State Mail Room Complex
Las Vegas, NV 89158
(702) 386-5293

New Hampshire

Consumer Protection and
Antitrust Division
Office of Attorney General
State House Annex
Concord, NH 03301
(603) 271-3641

New Jersey

Division of Consumer Affairs
Department of Law and Public Safety
1100 Raymond Boulevard
Room 504
Newark, NJ 07102
(201) 648-4010

New Mexico

Consumer and Economic Crime Division

Office of Attorney General
P.O. Box 1508
Santa Fe, NM 87503
(505) 982-6916

New York

New York Consumer Protection Bd.
99 Washington Avenue
Albany, NY 12210
(518) 474-8583

North Carolina

Special Deputy Attorney General
Consumer Protection Division
Department of Justice Building
P.O. Box 629
Raleigh, NC 27602
(919) 733-7741

North Dakota

Consumer Affairs Office
State Laboratories Department
P.O. Box 937
Bismarck, ND 58505
(701) 224-2485
(800) 472-2927 (North Dakota only)

Ohio

Consumer Frauds and Crimes Sectio
Office of Attorney General
30 East Broad Street
15th Floor
Columbus, OH 43215
(614) 466-8831 or 4986

(800) 282-0515 (Ohio only)

Oklahoma

Department of Complaints
Investigation and Mediation
Oklahoma Corporation Commission
Jim Thorpe Building
Room 680
Oklahoma City, OK 73105
(405) 521-4113

Oregon

Consumer Protection and
Services Division
Department of Justice
500 Pacific Building
520 SW Yamhill Street
Portland, OR 97204
(503) 229-5522

Pennsylvania

Bureau of Consumer Protection
Office of Attorney General
Strawberry Square
ISth Floor
Harrisburg, PA 17120
(717) 787-9707

Rhode Island

Rhode Island Consumers' Council
365 Broadway
Providence, RI 02909
(401) 277-2764

South Carolina

Department of Consumer Affairs
600 Columbia Building
P.O. Box 5757
Columbia, SC 29250
(803) 758-2040
(800) 922-1594

South Dakota

Division of Consumer Protection
Office of Attorney General
Insurance Building
Pierre, SD 57501
(605) 773-4400
(800) 592-1865

Tennessee

Division of Consumer Affairs
Box 40627 Melrose Station
Nashville, TN 37204
(615) 741-1461
(800) 342-8385

Texas

Assistant Attorney General
Consumer Protection
and Antitrust Division
Office of Attorney General
P.O. Box 12548, Capitol Station
Austin, TX 78711
(512) 475-3288

Washington

Consumer Protection
and Antitrust Division
Office of Attorney General
1366 Dexter Horton Building
Seattle, WA 98104
(206) 464-7744
(800) 552-0700

West Virginia

Consumer Protection Division
Office of Attorney General
1204 Kanawha Boulevard East
Charleston, WV 25301
(304) 348-8986

Wisconsin

Division of Trade
and Consumer Protection
Department of Agriculture, Trade
and Consumer Protection
P.O. Box 8911
801 West Badger Road
Madison, WI 53708
(608) 266-9837
(800) 362-3020

Appendix Five

Federal Trade Commission Offices

NATIONAL OFFICE

Correspondence Office
Federal Trade Commission
Washington, DC 20580
(202) 523-3567

REGIONAL OFFICES

Atlanta

> Alabama
> Florida
> Georgia
> Mississippi
> North Carolina
> South Carolina
> Tennessee
> Virginia

1718 Peachtree Street, N.W.
Suite 1000
Atlanta, GA 30367
(404) 881-4836

Boston

> Connecticut
> Maine
> Massachusetts
> New Hampshire
> Rhode Island
> Vermont

150 Causeway Street
Room 1301
Boston, MA 02114
(617) 223-6621

Chicago

> Illinois
> Indiana
> Iowa
> Kentucky
> Minnesota
> Missouri
> Wisconsin

55 E. Monroe Street
Suite 1437
Chicago, IL 60603
(312) 353-4423

Cleveland

> Delaware
> Maryland
> Michigan
> New York (w. of Rochester)
> Ohio
> Pennsylvania
> West Virginia

118 St. Claire Avenue
Suite 500
Cleveland, OH 44114
(216) 552-4207

Dallas

Arizona
Louisiana
New Mexico
Oklahoma
Texas

2001 Bryan Street
Suite 2665
Dallas, TX 75201
(214) 767-0032

Denver

Colorado
Kansas
Montana
Nebraska
North Dakota
South Dakota
Utah
Wyoming

1405 Curtis Street
Suite 2900
Denver, CO 80202
(303) 837-2271

Los Angeles

Arizona
Southern California

11000 Wilshire Boulevard
Los Angeles, CA 90024
(213) 824-7575

San Francisco

Hawaii
Nevada
Northern California

450 Golden Gate Avenue
San Francisco, CA 94102
(415) 556-1270

FTC Field Station
P.O. Box 50169
Honolulu, Hl 96850
(808) 546-5685

New York City

New Jersey
New York (east of Rochester)

26 Federal Plaza
Room 2243-EB
New York, NY 10278
(212) 264-1207

Seattle

Alaska
Idaho
Oregon
Washington

915 2nd Avenue
Seattle, WA 98174
(206) 442-4655

Appendix Six

Food and Drug Administration Office

National

Consumer Affairs and
Small Business Staff (HF0-22)
Food and Drug Administration
Dept. of Health and Human Services
5600 Fishers Lane
Room 13-82
Rockville, MD 20857
(301) 443-3170

Region I

Food and Drug Administration
585 Commercial Street
Boston, MA 02109
(617) 223-5857

Region II

Food and Drug Administration
20 Evergreen Place
East Orange, NJ 07018
(201) 645-6356

Food and Drug Administration
850 Third Avenue
Brooklyn, NY 11232
(212) 965-5754

Food and Drug Administration
599 Delaware Avenue
Buffalo, NY 14202
(716) 846-4461

Food and Drug Administration
P.O. Box 54427, Old San Juan Station
San Juan, PR 00905
(809) 723-4465

Region III

Food and Drug Administration
900 Madison Avenue
Baltimore, MD 21201
(301) 962-3593

Food and Drug Administration
U.S. Customhouse, Room 900
2nd and Chestnut Streets
Philadelphia, PA 19106
(215) 597-0837

Food and Drug Administration
Pittsburgh Resident Inspection Post
7 Parkway Center
Suite 645
Pittsburgh, PA 15220
(412) 644-2858

Food and Drug Administration
Falls Church Resident Inspection Po
701 W. Broad Street
Room 309
Falls Church, VA 22046
(703) 285-2578

Region IV

Food and Drug Administration
P.O. Box 118
Orlando, FL 32802
(305) 855-0900

Food and Drug Administration
1182 W. Peachtree Street, N.W.
Atlanta, GA 30309
(404) 881-7355

Food and Drug Administration
297 Plus Park Boulevard
Nashville, TN 37217
(615) 251-7127

Region V

Food and Drug Administration
433 West Van Buren Street
1222 Main Post Office Building
Chicago, IL 60607
(312) 353-7840

Food and Drug Administration
Indianapolis Resident Inspection Post
575 North Pennsylvania
Room 693
Indianapolis, IN 46204
(319) 269-6500

Food and Drug Administration
1560 East Jefferson Avenue
Detroit, Ml 48207
(313) 226-6260

Food and Drug Administration
240 Hennepin Avenue
Minneapolis, MN 55401

(612) 725-2121

Food and Drug Administration
1141 Central Parkway
Cincinnati, OH 45202
(513) 684-3501

Food and Drug Administration
U.S. Courthouse Building
85 Marconi Boulevard
Room 231
Columbus, OH 43215
(614) 4697353

Food and Drug Administration
Cleveland Resident Inspection Post
601 Rockwell Avenue
Room 453
Cleveland, OH 44114
(216) 5224844

Food and Drug Administration
Milwaukee Resident Inspection Post
615 E. Michigan Street
Milwaukee, Wl 53202
(414) 2913904

Region VI

Food and Drug Administration
500 South Ervay
Suite 470B
Dallas, TX 75201
(214) 7675433

Food and Drug Administration
4298 Elysian Fields Avenue

New Orleans, LA 70122
(504) 5896344

Food and Drug Administration
Houston Station
1440 N. Loop
Suite 250
Houston, TX 77009
(713) 2265581

Food and Drug Administration
San Antonio Resident Inspection Post
419 S. Main
Room 301
San Antonio, TX 78204
(512) 2296737

Region VII

Food and Drug Administration
1009 Cherry Street
Kansas City, MO 64106
(816) 3745623

Food and Drug Administration
St. Louis Station
Laclete's Landing
80B North Collins Street
St. Louis, MO 63102
(314) 4254137

Food and Drug Administration
Omaha Resident Inspection Post
1619 Howard Street
Omaha, NE 68102
(402) 2214676

Region VIII

Food and Drug Administration
500 U.S. Customhouse
19th and California Streets
Denver, CO 80202
(303) 8374915

Region IX

Food and Drug Administration
50 United Nations Plaza
Room 518
San Francisco, CA 94102
(415) 5562682

Food and Drug Administration
1521 W. Pico Boulevard
Los Angeles, CA 90015
(213) 6883771

Region X

Food and Drug Administration
909 First Avenue
Federal Office Building
Room 5003
Seattle, WA 98174
(206) 4425310

Appendix Seven

U.S. Consumer Product Safety Commission Offices

Atlanta Regional Office

    Alabama

    Florida

    Georgia

    Kentucky

    Mississippi

    North Carolina

    South Carolina

    Tennessee

Consumer Product Safety Commission
1330 West Peachtree Street, N.W.
Atlanta, GA 30309
(404) 881-2231

Boston Regional Office

    Connecticut

    Massachusetts

    Maine

    New Hampshire

    Rhode Island

    Vermont

Consumer Product Safety Commission
100 Summer Street
Room 1607
Boston, MA 02110
(617) 223-5576

Chicago Regional Office

    Illinois

    Indiana

    Minnesota

    Wisconsin

Consumer Product Safety Comn.
230 S. Dearborn Street
Room 2945
Chicago, IL 60604
(312) 353-8260

Twin Cities District Office

Consumer Product Safety Comn.
Metro Square,
Suite 580
7th and Robert
Saint Paul, MN 55101
(612) 725-7781

Cleveland Regional Office

    Michigan

    Ohio

Consumer Product Safety Comn.
Plaza Nine Building
Room 520
55 Erieview Plaza
Cleveland, OH 44114
(216) 522-3886

Kansas City Regional Office

    Colorado

    Iowa

    Kansas

    Missouri

    Montana

    Nebraska

    North Dakota

    South Dakota

    Utah

    Wyoming

Consumer Product Safety Commission
Midland Building
Suite 1000
1221 Baltimore Avenue
Kansas City, MO 64105
(816) 374-2034

Denver District Office

Consumer Product Safety Commission
Guaranty Bank Building
Suite 938
817 17th Street
Denver, CO 80202
(303) 837-2904

Los Angeles Regional Office

    Arizona

    Southern California

Consumer Product Safety Commission
3660 Wilshire Boulevard
Suite 1100
Los Angeles, CA 90010
(213) 688-7272

New York Regional Office

    New Jersey

    New York

    Puerto Rico

    Virgin Islands

Consumer Product Safety Comn.
6 World Trade Center
Vesey Street
6th Floor
New York, NY 10048
(212) 264-1125

Philadelphia Regional Office

    Delaware

    Washington, D.C.

    Maryland

    Pennsylvania

    Virginia

    West Virginia

Consumer Product Safety Comn.
400 Market Street
10th Floor
Philadelphia, PA 19106
(215) 597-9105

San Francisco Regional Office

    Alaska

    Hawaii

    Idaho

    Nevada

    Northern California

    Oregon

    Washington

Consumer Product Safety Commmission
U.S. Customs House
555 Battery Street
Room 416
San Francisco, CA 94111
(415) 556-1816

Seattle District Office
Consumer Product Safety Commission
3240 Federal Building
915 Second Avenue
Seattle, WA 98174
(206) 442-5276

Appendix Eight

Automotive Company Addresses

Acura

Customer Relations
Acura
1919 Torrance Blvd.
Torrance, CA 90501

Audi

Consumer Relations Office
Audi
888 West Big Beaver Road
Troy, MI 48007
(800) 822-8987

BMW

National Customer Relations Manager
BMW
P.O. Box 1227
Westwood, NJ 07675
(201) 307-4000

Buick

Customer Assistance
Buick
902 East Hamilton Avenue
Flint, Ml 48550
(800) 521-7300

Cadillac

Consumer Relations Center
Cadillac
2860 Clark Street
Detroit, Ml 48232
(800) 458-8006

Chevrolet-Geo Motor Division

Customer Relations Department
P.O. Box 7047
Troy, MI 48007
(800) 222-1020

Chrysler

Customer Relations
Chrysler Corporation
P.O. Box 1718
Detroit, MI 48288
(800) 992-1997

Daihatsu

Consumer Relations Office
Daihatsu
4422 Corporate Center Drive
Los Alamados, CA 90720
(800) 777-7070

Dodge

Customer Relations
Chrysler Corporation
P.O. Box 1718
Detroit, MI 48288
(800) 992-1997

Eagle

Customer Relations
Chrysler Corporation
P.O. Box 1718
Detroit, MI 48288
(800) 992-1997

Honda Motor Company

Corporate Office
Customer Relations Supervisor
American Honda Motor Company, Inc.
100 West Alondra Blvd.
Gardena, CA 90247
(213) 327-8280

Hyundai

Consumer Affairs
10550 Talbert Avenue
Fountain Valley, CA 92728
(714) 890-6242

Infiniti

Customer Relations
Infiniti

18701 Figueroa Street
Carson, CA 90248
(213) 532-3111

Isuzu

Consumer Relations
Isuzu
P.O. Box 2480
City of Industry, CA 91746
(800) 255-6727

Jeep

Customer Relations
Chrysler Corporation
P.O. Box 1718
Detroit, MI 48288
(800) 992-1997

Ford Motor Company

Customer Assistance Center
Ford Motor Company
P.O. Box 43360
Detroit, Ml 48243
(800) 392-3673

Lexus

Lexus Customer Satisfaction Center
19001 South Western Avenue
Torrance, CA 90509
(800) 872-5398

Mazda Motors

Mazda Customer Service
P.O. 19734
Irvine, CA 92713
(714) 727-1990

Mercedes-Benz

Corporate Office
Owner Services
Mercedes-Benz of North America, Inc.
One Mercedes Drive
Montvale, NJ 07645
(201) 573-0600

Mercury

Customer Assistance Center
Ford Motor Company
P.O. Box 43360
Detroit, Ml 48243
(800) 392-3673

Mitsubishi

Consumer Relations
Mitsubishi
6400 Katella Avenue
Cypress, CA 90630
(714) 372-6000

Nissan

1860 Figueroa Street
Carson, CA 90248

Consumer Assistance
Nissan

(800) 647-7261

Oldsmobile

Customer Assistance Office
Oldsmobile
905 Southland
Lansing, Ml 48910
(800) 442-6537

Peugeot

Peugeot Consumer Relations
One Peugeot Plaza
Lyndhurst, NJ 07071
(201) 935-8400

Plymouth

Customer Relations
Chrysler Corporation
P.O. Box 1718
Detroit, MI 48288
(800) 992-1997

Pontiac

Customer Assistance
Pontiac
One Pontiac Plaza
Pontiac, Ml 48053
(800) 762-2737

Range Rover

Customer Service
Range Rover
4390 Parliament Place
P.O. Box 1503
Lanham, MD 20706
(800) 637-6837

Saturn

Saturn Assistance Center
P.O. Box 1500
Highway 31 South
Spring Hill, TN 37174
(800) 553-6000

Sterling

Consumer Affairs
Sterling
8300 N.W. 53rd Street
Suite 200
Miami, FL 33166
(305) 597-6500

Suburu

Consumer Relations
7040 Central Highway
Pennsauken, NJ 08109
(800) 932-0636

Suzuki

Customer Relations
Suzuki

3251 E. Imperial Highway
Brea, CA 92621
(714) 996-7040

Volkswagen

Customer Relations
888 West Big Beaver Road
Troy, MI 48007
(800) 822-8987

Volvo

Consumer Affairs Manager
Volvo
One Volvo Drive
Rockleigh, NJ 07647
(800) 458-1552

Appendix Nine

Auto Consumer Action Programs

Arizona

Arizona Automobile Dealers
AUTOCAP
P.O. Box 5438
Phoenix, AZ 85010
(602) 252-2386

California

Motor Car Dealers of So. California
AUTOCAP
420 W. Culver Blvd.
Playa Del Rey, CA 90293
(800) 722-0579 (In state)
(213) 301-1554 (Out of state)

San Diego Motor Car Dealers
AUTOCAP
2525 Camino Del Rio South
Suite 103
San Diego, CA 92108
(619 296-2265

Colorado

Colorado Automobile Dealers
AUTOCAP
1601 Emerson Street
Denver, CO 80218
(303) 831-1722

Connecticut
See New York

District of Columbia

Automotive Trade Association of
the National Capital Area
AUTOCAP
15873 Crabbs Branch Way
Rockville, MD 20855
(301) 670-1110
(Washington, D.C.; Northern Virgini
Montgomery and Prince Georges
Counties, MD only)

Florida

Jacksonville Automobile Dealers
AUTOCAP
3100 University Blvd.
Suite 239
Jacksonville, FL 32216
(904) 721-2339 (Duval County only)

South Florida Automobile Dealers
AUTOCAP
16291 N.W. 57th Avenue
Miami, FL 33014
(305) 624-1828 (Dade & Monroe Cou
(305) 522-2886 (Broward County)

AUTOCAP
2247 Palm Beach Lakes Blvd.
Suite 211
West Palm Beach, FL 33409
(407) 686-6168 (West Palm Beach)
(407) 272-4445 (Boca Raton & DelRay)

Georgia

Ceorgia Automobile Dealers
AUTOCAP
4000 Cumberland Parkway
Building 900, Suite A
Atlanta, GA 30339
(404) 432-1658

Hawaii

Hawaii Automobile Dealers
AUTOCAP
7 Waterfront Plaza
500 Ala Moana Blvd.
Kailua, Hl 96813
(808) 526-0159

Illinois

Illinois New Car and Truck Dealers
AUTOCAP
828 South Second Street
P.O. Box 3045
Springfield, IL 62708
(217) 753-4513

Kentucky

Kentucky Automobile Dealers
AUTOCAP

181 St. Ann Street
Lexington, KY 40502
(606) 268-6636

Maine

Maine Automobile Dealers
AUTOCAP
P.O. Box 2667
Augusta, ME 04330
(207) 623-3882

Maryland
See District of Columbia

Michigan

Michigan Automobile Dealers
AUTOCAP
P.O. Box 2525
East Lansing, Ml 48823
(800) 292-1923 (In state)
(517) 351-7800 (Out of state)
(Does not cover Macomb,
Oakland or Wayne Counties)

Montana

Montana Automobile Dealers
AUTOCAP
501 N. Sanders
Helena, MT 59601
(406) 442-1233

New Hampshire

New Hampshire Automobile Dealers
AUTOCAP
P.O. Box 2337
Concord, NH 03302
(603) 224-2369

New Mexico

New Mexico Automobile and
Truck Dealers Association
AUTOCAP
3815 Hawkins N.E.
Albuquerque, NM 87109
(505) 345-6060

New York

Broome County Chamber of Commerce
AUTOCAP
P.O. Box 995
Binghamton, NY 13902
(607) 723-7127
(Broome County only)

Capital District Automobile Dealers
AUTOCAP
125 Wolf Road, Suite 501
Albany, NY 12205
(518) 438-0584
(Albany, Saratoga, Schenectady
and Troy Counties only)

Niagara Frontier Automobile Dealers
AUTOCAP
1144 Wehrle Drive
Williamsville, NY 14221

(716) 631-8510
(Niagara County only)

Rochester Automobile Dealers
AUTOCAP
2024 W. Henrietta Road, Building 4
Rochester, NY 14623
(716) 272-7232

Greater N.Y. Automobile Dealers
AUTOCAP
18-10 Whitestone Expressway
Whitestone, NY 11357
(800) 522-3881
(Serves New York City, Long Island,
Westchester)

New York State Automobile Dealers
AUTOCAP
37 Elk Street
P.O. Box 7287
Albany, NY 12224
(800) 342-9208 (In state)
(518) 463-1148 (Out of state)
(Serves balance of state)

North Carolina

North Carolina Automobile Dealers
P.O. Box 12167
Raleigh, NC 26705
(919) 828-4427

North Dakota
Automobile Dealers Association
AUTOCAP
P.O. Box 2524
Fargo, ND 58108

(701) 293-6822

Ohio

Cleveland Automobile Dealers
AUTOCAP
6100 Rockside Woods Blvd.
Suite 235
Independence, OH 44131
(216) 328-1500
(Metropolitan Cleveland only)

Ohio Automobile Dealers Association
1366 Dublin Road
Columbus, OH 43215
(614) 487-1400

Oklahoma

Tulsa Automobile Dealers Association
525 S. Main Street, Suite 201
Tulsa, OK 74103
(918) 587-0141
(Metropolitan Tulsa only)

Oregon

Oregon Automobile Dealers Association
AUTOCAP
P.O. Box 14460
Portland, OR 97214
(503) 233-5044

Rhode Island

Rhode Island Automobile Dealers
335D Centerville Road
Warwick, RI 02886

(401) 732-6870

South Carolina

South Carolina Automobile
and Truck Dealers Association
AUTOCAP
1517 Laurel Street
Columbia, SC 29201
(803) 254-4040

South Dakota

South Dakota Automobile Dealers
AUTOCAP
P.O. Box 80540
Sioux Falls, SD 57116
(605) 336-2616

Texas

Texas Automobile Dealers Associati
AUTOCAP
1108 Lavaca
P.O. Box 1028
Austin, TX 78767
(512) 476-2686

Vermont

Vermont Automotive Trade Associat
AUTOCAP
P.O. Box 561
Montpelier, VT 05602
(800) 642-5149 (In state)

Virginia

Automotive Trade Association
of the National Capital Area
(Northern Virginia only
See District of Columbia)

Virginia Automobile Dealers Association
AUTOCAP
P.O. Box 5407
Richmond, VA 23220
(804) 359-3578
(Serves balance of state)

Wisconsin

Wisconsin Automobile & Truck Dealers
Association
P.O. Box 5345
Madison, WI 53705
(608) 251-3023

Index

About the Authors

Arlene Singer earned her BA degree in psychology at American University. She has been a professional buyer for fifteen years in the advertising field. In addition, Ms. Singer is the mother of three, responsible for purchasing and returning clothing and gadgets for an active family. Arlene lives with her husband and children in the Washington, D.C. area.

Karen Parmet earned her BA degree in sociology at UCLA. She assisted Robert J. Ringer when he wrote the bestselling book *Winning Through Intimidation*. Karen has shopped (and returned) at every major, and many minor, stores on both coasts. A native of Los Angeles, Ms. Parmet now lives in the Washington, D.C. area with her husband and three children.